GETTING FROM YOU AND ME TO WE

A GUIDE TO BUILDING LASTING RELATIONSHIPS AND ALLIANCES

CHARLES H. NEWMAN

Copyright © 2012 by CHARLES H. NEWMAN

All rights reserved. No part of this book may be reproduced or transmitted in any form or by any means, electronic or mechanical, including photocopying, recording, or by any information storage and retrieval system, without permission in writing from the copyright owner.

This book was printed in the United States of America.

To order additional copies of this book, contact:

www.CreateSpace.com/3987740

ISBN: 1479263079

ISBN 13: 9781479263073

Dedication

In memory of Jeremy Winer who taught me that there is more to life than work, that each day you go fishing adds one day to your life and that the only thing we get to take with us are our memories. So Jeremy, my friend, thanks for the memories. You may be gone, but you never will be forgotten.

Table of Contents

Dedication v

Acknowledgements ix

Preface xi

Introduction. xiii

Chapter 1 – Relationships and Alliances .1

Chapter 2 – Initial Steps 5

   Chicken Dance Meets Mexican Hat Dance *26*

   Chicken Dance, Chicken Ranch or Mustang Ranch? *29*

   The Ultimate Chicken Dance *31*

   How the Chicken Got to the Dining Table *34*

Chapter 3 – Cultural Snapshots 37

Chapter 4 – Everything in Life Is Negotiable. 43

   Everybody Wins *71*

   A Touch of Creativity Mixed with a Bit of Humor *73*

   Another Shopping Adventure. *74*

   Creating Opportunities and Saving Money. *76*

   Try It; It Works. *78*

   Why You Need All the Information *80*

   Information Is Power. *82*

   The More Information, the Better the Outcome. *83*

The Clock Strikes Again. *84*
The Key to Better and Longer Lasting Relationships. *85*
Win-Win Is A Lifestyle for Success *87*
The Deal Maker *91*
Know When to Fold and When to Run *92*
50 Ways to Leave the Negotiating Table *94*
The Ultimate Negotiation. *96*
Are Negotiations Ever Over? *99*

Chapter 5 – Everybody Wins 105

Epilogue 115

Acknowledgements

The people who have contributed to this book are far too numerous to mention by name. Nevertheless, credit has to be given to Ford Motor Company which had enough confidence to allow me to put together a variety of business alliances around the world. It would be unfair not to acknowledge everyone who sat patiently and enduringly at the table with me while we negotiated and to build the long lasting personal relationships and business alliances.

Sadly, some of these alliances did not survive more than a few years, but they did serve a useful business purpose while in existence. Other alliances survived much longer, and served both parties well, despite the hurdles and frustrations the businesses and the people met with along the way. The personal relationships and friendships formed as a result of these undertakings have survived longer than many of the alliances themselves. From that standpoint, all of these efforts have value and can be considered successful.

To all who were involved, thank you for your patience, your understanding, your good will and your efforts in supporting these undertakings and in helping them succeed. I now realize that I was enlightened and enriched by each of you and for that I also thank you all.

A special thanks to my friend, Jim Pagano who contributed much of his time and talent to the creative aspects of this book as well as my earlier publication, *Beyond the Chicken Dance*.

Finally, much of the credit for this book must go to my wife Arlene. She has spent countless hours tirelessly listening to the negotiating stories. She also has provided her creative and artistic talents to the finished product. Most of all, she has been patient and has supported my efforts to complete this book.

Preface

As we go through life, there are some people and experiences that have such a great impact on our lives we can recall them clearly and vividly. I am fortunate to have had the opportunity to meet and develop great friendships with people who challenge me, enlighten me, and inspire me not only to reach my potential, but to help others reach theirs. This book is written by one of those people and I am honored to have the opportunity to be a part of sharing it with you.

I met Charlie several years ago through a mutual friend, Reno Lovison, author of Turn Your Business Card into Business and founder of Authors Broadcast. Reno and I were talking after a radio show interview when he told me there was someone I absolutely had to meet. Reno thought this person would be a great guest for National Entrepreneurs Network's live internet TV show. He said his name is Charlie Newman and he traveled all over the world negotiating for Ford Motor Company and other businesses. Charlie had just written a great book about his experiences entitled Beyond the Chicken Dance. That definitely intrigued me.

A few weeks later, Charlie and I were in our studio chatting before the show. I have to say it was one of the most entertaining shows we did. Charlie has a wealth of experience and has the stories to go with it. He is the kind of person that quickly connects with everyone. In this book, Charlie shares some great stories, lessons learned, and experiences that changed the direction of his life and may just change yours.

I remember when he first started talking about writing this book. He and I were sitting outside a little coffee shop on a beautiful sunny day in Vero Beach, Florida. It had been many months since we last had the opportunity to catch up and I had driven down for the morning to pick up some autographed copies of his first book, Beyond the Chicken Dance, for some of my clients. As he shared what he had in mind for this book, I was hooked. Now that I have read the final draft, I know you will be too.

Once again, Charlie draws on his experiences and, through real life stories, leads us to recognize that we are building relationships every day of our lives. He then provides us with some very powerful tips to make each of our experiences less stressful and more rewarding.

As you read this book, you will be engaged, entertained, and empowered to build better relationships. Charlie is truly a master of *Getting From You and Me to WE*.

Thomas Fulmer
CEO, Success Essentials Training & Coaching
Founder, National Entrepreneurs Network
Founder, Mobile Phone Marketing Solutions

Introduction

This book brings you real life experiences. It focuses on creative collaboration. Its purpose is to give you a head start in building better and longer lasting relationships – those that teach you lifetime lessons. Your job is to accept those lessons and put what you have learned to use in all areas of your life. My job is to give you some quick tips to help you do so. Simply put, that is the reason I wrote this book.

The book will help you build and manage your relationships in a way that will increase your chances of success over the long term. It will enlighten you as to what takes place every time people meet. It will provide you with a series of negotiating stories to reinforce what it takes to achieve more satisfactory results. Finally, it will provide you with 16 easy-to-use, power negotiating tips that every successful negotiator knows and uses.

This book builds upon the information provided in my earlier book, *Beyond the Chicken Dance*. By applying the guidelines in this book, you can avoid many of the mistakes made by others resulting in more rewarding relationships and better outcomes in your personal life as well as your business dealings.

The main thing that I've taken away from every relationship is that there is one constant, and that constant is change. No matter what the parties envision from the outset, things have a way of changing. People change and their positioning relative to one another changes. The better prepared you are to deal with these changes, the better your chance of success.

Professor Srinivasa Rangan of Babson College stated this following about *Beyond the Chicken Dance:*

"....... this book is about life itself." Recognizing that almost everything is negotiable, understanding what motivates others, and maintaining flexibility in the face of potential changes in circumstances are life lessons that anyone can benefit from."

Getting from You and Me to WE takes it one step further. It provides you with additional negotiating tips and more real life stories to help you reinforce your skills and build longer lasting relationships.

CHAPTER 1

RELATIONSHIPS AND ALLIANCES

Understanding what motivates people and understanding how to deal with changing circumstances are key to successful, longer lasting relationships. By the time you finish this book you should have gained significant insights on: (1) how to form more productive relationships to the benefit of all parties, (2) how to improve your negotiating skills and (3) how to manage alliances and friendships for life.

According to the New Oxford American Dictionary, a relationship is defined as "the way in which two or more people or organizations regard and behave toward each other." It defines an alliance as "a union or association formed for mutual benefit" or "a relationship based on an affinity in interests, nature or qualities." As you read this book keep these definitions in mind with particular emphasis on how "people or organizations regard and behave toward each other."

While some aspects of this book such as the negotiating guidelines outlined in Chapter 4 may apply, the focus of this book is not on "one off" transactions like stopping impulsively to buy an ice cream. This book focuses on situations where an ongoing relationship is anticipated. As such, both party's have to: (1) trust each other, (2) believe that they have gained some of what they wanted and (3) feel good about the interaction and the outcome.

A business alliance is a formal association of two or more parties to further their common interests, presumably over the long term. As such, these alliances can take many forms with varying degrees of complexity and difficulty. In its simplest form, an alliance can be described as a long term buy-sell arrangement. On a more complex level, a long term relationship and alliance may result from an effort to codevelop or share technology, or perhaps a technology licensing agreement. Even more complex are partnerships or joint ventures. Joint ventures represent the ultimate level of complexity, particularly when the global aspect of business is introduced. If the parties to the alliance are from different countries and different cultures, the relationship can become inherently more complex.

Unfortunately, there are too many examples of alliances formed between business entities that were predicated upon the premise that "everyone else in the industry is doing it, so it must be the right course of action." Others have been formed based upon some whim of upper-level management with no real analysis whether an alliance was really necessary. In almost all cases where inadequate planning superseded the formation of the relationship, the likelihood of success was diminished and the likelihood of failure was practically guaranteed. In almost every regard, this concept applies equally as well to personal relationships. When relationships are rushed into, they often fail.

In contrast, when properly developed and formed, long term relationships and alliances represent an opportunity to benefit from the expertise of each party, thereby creating a more powerful platform than one based on the experience and expertise of an individual. It is critical in personal relationships. It becomes even more critical in today's global business environment wherein the right partner can provide knowledge of unique legal requirements, local business practices, customs, and other nuances tailored to the specific market.

Relationships and Alliances

Before attempting to form an alliance, you need to make sure that you are familiar with the steps. Preparing in advance is like practicing the steps before your first dance. It will help you avoid possible costly mistakes, and perhaps help you avoid stepping on someone's toes.

You need to answer the following questions before you take that first dance step:

1. Do we truly need an alliance or do we have the expertise and resources required to succeed on our own?
2. What benefits are expected from an alliance versus going it alone (both financial and non-financial)?
3. With whom should we establish a long term relationship? Who are the best potential alliance associates?
4. What alternative forms of alliance have been considered and what form should the alliance take?

To answer these questions you will need to do a thorough, objective and honest assessment of your company's business environment, the internal and external challenges it faces, its resource capabilities and limitations, AND its strengths and its weaknesses. You also will want to evaluate the opportunities and threats facing your business. To complete this assessment, you need a detailed plan.

I am sure you have heard the story about the one house in the neighborhood with the unkempt lawn belonging to the guy who owns the landscape business. Well, I must admit that I have followed the same path. For a number of years I went around the world preaching "planning" and "if you do not write it down, you will never do it." During those years my wife and I failed to develop and implement a plan for ourselves. I am not referring to a financial plan, but one I would call a "plan for life."

It turned out to be simple and fun. Here is all it takes. Draw a line down the middle of an 8 1/2 X 11" piece of paper. On one side, put the heading "Things I Want to Do." On the other side put the heading, "Places I Want to Go." Give a copy to your partner.

My wife and I agreed to limit each side of the page to ten items. We also agreed that one week later we would sit down to compare and consolidate the lists. We have been working on our consolidated "Bucket List" for several years now and have enjoyed discovering each other's new list of "wants."

We have gone hot air ballooning, I have flown a WWII P-51 Mustang and she has taken art classes. In addition, we have traveled extensively alternating between her "wants" and mine. We update the lists regularly and always have something new to look forward to doing together. The point is, previously we had talked about these things, but just kept putting them off. Once we wrote them down, we planned for them and started crossing them off the list one at a time. Our only concern is what happens when there are no more items on the list. As a result, we just keep adding to it and having more fun together.

What it entails is a simple idea and one that can help build a better relationship. You should try it! Not only will you get better focused, but you will have a partner who is an integral part of the process, a partner who gets to input their "wants" into the plan, and what is more important, you will have a partner who buys into the plan.

Now, let's go on to the initial steps to ensure that any future efforts you undertake to establish relationships have the potential to be better than if you had gone to the dance without understanding these steps.

CHAPTER 2

INITIAL STEPS

This chapter could just as easily been entitled "Getting to Know You" as it is the beginning stage for all relationships, both personal and business. You may not have thought about it in these terms, but you already have been involved in this dance many times throughout your personal life as well as your professional career.

The "chicken dance" is a phrase I've used in numerous situations to describe the actions and antics people use to maneuver themselves into better position so they can gain something such as control, power, money or anything else of perceived value. It goes on all the time and it goes on at all levels. Typically it peaks during the early stages of any gathering when people perceive they have something to gain from the outcome of the discussions.

Although, at the time, I didn't recognize it as the "chicken dance," my earliest recollection of learning the steps took place in the poolroom where I spent much of my youth. To be truthful about it, I probably spent twice as many hours in the poolroom as I did in high school. To me it was just a different education, but what a useful learning experience it turned out to be! I am convinced the lessons I learned in that environment provided the foundation for learning how to deal with people from different cultures. If you have ever been to, or read a story about, an old-fashioned poolroom, you can imagine the characters you may have met there.

If you have time, take a look at the movie "The Hustler," which will allow you to watch the "chicken dance" unfold. Another excellent portrayal of the "chicken dance" can be seen in the positioning that takes place among the "seven kingdoms" in the HBO series entitled "Game of Thrones." Finally, Donald Trump's program "The Apprentice," which is featured on Sunday nights on NBC TV, clearly illustrates all three elements of this book. It clearly shows the chicken dance that people undertake to gain position and power, (2) it shows the changing nature of relationships to add value and (3) it enables you to see a variety of negotiating techniques both good and bad. One positive aspect is that you can observe this taking place in a real world competitive environment. Better yet, you can watch the human behavior, the relationships and the tactics intensify as the season progresses.

The first "chicken dance" I recall happened when I was a very young looking thirteen or fourteen year old. At the time, I had been shooting pool for the better part of two or three years. Like most activities, the more hours of practice, the better your performance. Since I was averaging four to six hours daily, six days a week, my game was good.

One afternoon I was hanging around practicing a few shots when some of the "older" guys challenged me to a game of "nine ball," where the balls have to be shot in numerical order. The 5 ball and the 9 ball are the "money" balls. After I had beaten each of them a few times, I must have completed a rite of passage. Apparently, I was good enough for some of the older guys—older being around 20 years of age — to back me against unsuspecting newcomers. I really had arrived when I was officially dubbed "The Count," a nickname I carry to this day.

My three primary backers were Dick "the Clock," Paulie "the Rat" and Larry "the Snake." Each of them always had money, but never

Initial Steps

seemed to work. They always were hanging around the poolroom conjuring up creative ways to make money. Watching these three work the people who came through the door was a thing of beauty. They would provide a running commentary, on each game on each table, as they circulated looking for easy targets. They would compliment some of the lesser skilled players as a way to bolster the players' egos. Others, who appeared to be fairly good, often were the subject of criticism and sometimes harsh remarks intended to rile them up. Of course, the object was to get a challenge from one of the players to "put up or shut up!" That's when I just happened to show up.

At that point, "The Clock," "The Rat" or "The Snake," contingent upon who was orchestrating the dance, would put me into the equation. Typically, I'd be standing by the candy counter or watching a game on another table when I'd hear, "Hey, kid, do you want to shoot a game?" Naturally, I already had learned the dance steps and very innocently would allow myself to get suckered into a game with someone I had been watching out of the corner of my eye.

It would play out by my losing the first few of games. Then the bets would increase slightly at which time the games would go back and forth, with the other party being slightly ahead. Then the bets would continue to increase as would the number of games I would begin to win. At some point the other party would end up playing for "double or nothing," which is when somehow I finally would grasp the finer points of the game and starting winning them all. It must have appeared to some of my opponents as pure luck as I would barely win. Unbelievably, these guys would come back a few days later, or the following week, with their friend to beat that baby-faced kid who got lucky last time around. At the end of the day, "The Clock," the "Rat" and the "Snake" would add up the winnings and I would get a cut. The next day we would return for another twirl on the dance floor with some new dance partners.

There are two lessons I learned from that time in my life. First, in the poolroom everyone is a "hustler" of one kind or another. Second, no matter how good you think you are, there always is someone who is better than you and eventually you are going to meet up with that person.

While the poolroom was interesting, there is no better place to observe the "chicken dance" than during negotiations. I even discovered that there are exceptions to my belief that everything in life is negotiable. While rare, they do occur. Most of the exceptions I have seen took place in the military, but even there, some things are negotiable. One instance in particular stands out. It is a good illustration of how the chicken dance works and how almost everything in life is negotiable, at least to some extent.

In 1958, I was assigned to the weather group attached to the Fifth Air Force Headquarters in Fuchu, Japan. In early 1959 I had reached the rank of sergeant. One morning I was called in to see my commanding officer. Colonel Nice Guy advised me that I was being considered for a special assignment. As the assignment required the highest level of security clearance, it would require my passing an extensive FBI background check. He then told me that if I passed the background check, I would be allowed behind the "steel door." Once there, I would be told the specifics of the assignment, but not before. Until that time I would not be told anything about it. Once told, however, I could never tell anyone else what we did behind that "steel door." Finally, Colonel Nice Guy told me, if I passed the background check and took the assignment, I could not be released from active duty until the assignment had been completed.

I only had about nine months remaining before I was to be released from active duty and returned home, and the colonel must have seen a question cross my face. At the time, I was standing in front of the colonel's desk, I was demonstrating my best military composure, but my face must have turned pale or my jaw dropped. It was a dead giveaway that I was concerned and confused. I did not have a good poker face at that point; I was worried that I was getting suckered into something. I was thinking that I was committing to something blindly. Being in the military, however, I believed the terms were not negotiable. I was told that I was going to be checked out by the FBI and if I passed, I would be reassigned. That was the end of discussion. As I was a 20 year old sergeant who believed anything was possible, I jumped in with both feet. I enthusiastically said I was proud to be considered for

Initial Steps

the assignment and would do my best at completing it, not if, but when I passed the FBI investigation.

About two months later, I returned to Colonel Nice Guy's office and was given my orders to report to the major in charge behind the "steel door." Upon arriving at the "steel door," I reported in by telephone. After identifying myself in about six different ways, I was allowed to enter. Next I was introduced to the rest of the team. The team included Major Serious, Lieutenant College Graduate, Master Sergeant Old-timer another sergeant like me, and me—the "New Kid." I was then briefed on my new duty assignment. Lastly, I was indoctrinated on a series of very rigid security policies and procedures. Of particular importance was the fact that there were only five people who worked in our group, including me. Also, only six other personnel in the entire Fifth Air Force Command were allowed access behind "the steel door." No other personnel, no matter their need, their rank, or their reasons were ever to be allowed access.

While the specific punishment for breaching this security provision was not explained in detail, it sounded as though the offender might never again see daylight. Put simply, it convinced me that if your name was not on the list, you would never get behind the "steel door" while I was on duty.

Major Serious also decided I would be an excellent candidate to work the "morning shift," which at the time sounded good to me. It sounded good until the major told me that morning is "0000 hours until 0600 hours" or midnight until 6:00 a.m. If that were not enough, that shift only required one person on duty so I would be working by myself. The good news was that I had a special pass to the mess hall and could eat any time I wanted, day or night. Also, because of the intensity of the work, I only worked four shifts a week. To me that was not so bad. My work week was composed of 24 hours total and I could eat any time I wanted. Now all I had to do was complete the assignment within about six to seven months so I could return home on time. Again, I believed nothing was negotiable, it came down from the top, as it always does in the military and many other large organizations, and living close to the bottom of the valley meant "making it happen."

Finally, Major Serious outlined the do's and don'ts governing the "steel door," behind which I now worked:

Rule #1. Only authorized personnel were allowed to enter. A list of ten people, including me, was posted on the inside of the door, and only those people were to be allowed inside.

Rule #2 The door had a combination lock imbedded in it like a giant walk-in bank vault. The combination would be changed at random times. You had to memorize it and never tell it to anyone else.

Rule #3. There were telephones on the inside and the outside of the door. You always communicated with people by phone and never opened the door until you were certain they were allowed access. Finally, there was a slit window in the door with bulletproof glass so the person on the other side of the door could be identified before being allowed in.

Rule #4. You always watched the person to whom you were talking and checked their identification cards through the window, even if you thought you knew the person.

Rule #5. There were weapons behind the door. If someone tried to force their way in, you must stop them any way you could.

Rule #6. If you ever allowed access to an unauthorized person, you would tried in a military court and the penalty would be severe.

Rule #7. You never could tell anyone what we were doing behind the "steel door." You would be watched and tested. If you ever disclosed what we were doing, you would be given a court-martial and the penalty would be severe.

About that time there was only one thought going through my head. I was thinking I had really been stupid. I had agreed to do something without having access to full information. I had agreed to do something without being able to negotiate any of the terms. Effectively, I had been given only limited information up front. I was not told enough to make an educated decision. In the military things are done differently and mostly for good reason. I later understood that there was no other way in this situation, but

Initial Steps

I learned a lesson I never forgot. That lesson is: Information is power, and if one party has it all, most likely you are going to end up with a less than optimum outcome.

That is not the end of the story, however. I paid very close attention to Major Serious as he went over the rules, and I made sure that I knew and understood them. There was no way I was going to break any of the rules and spend time in a military prison. Three or four months later, the phone rang about 0400 hours (4 o'clock in the morning). I picked up the telephone and peered out the sliding glass window, strictly following rules #3 and

#4. A Captain Perfection was on the outside of the door. He advised me he was the aide de camp to General SOB, who needed immediate access to the secure telephone behind the "steel door."

General SOB was standing about three feet behind Captain Perfection. Although the conversation with me had just begun, General SOB appeared to be getting impatient. He was standing with his arms folded across his chest while glaring at the "steel door." I wasn't entirely sure, but at the time I thought maybe generals could burn their way through steel if they glared long and hard enough.

Neither Captain Perfection nor General SOB were on the list of ten people with approved access. According to rule #1, I refused to let them in. Captain Perfection advised General SOB that I would not let him in. The truth was that a lowly sergeant was telling a general to go to hell. At that point, I thought the general would explode. His face went from red to purple. The veins stood out on his neck and he grabbed the telephone from Captain Perfection's hand. While General SOB continued to go a deeper shade of purple, Captain Perfection lost all of his color and went completely white. This was a new chicken dance to me and I was not sure of the steps.

General SOB then ordered me to give him instant access, which I again denied. He told me to give him my name, rank and serial number, which he repeated so Captain Perfection could write them down. I was getting nervous. I was beginning to think I had bought myself a one way ticket to military prison, but there was no way I was going to open the door. General SOB then shouted through the phone. He asked what I would do if he and his aide were to force their way in behind the door. Without hesitation, I said, "Sir, I'm going to call the Corporal of the Guard."

I don't think General SOB was expecting that answer as he looked very puzzled. After a pause, he asked, "Why the hell would you call the Corporal of the Guard?" "Sir," I answered, "I'm calling the Corporal of the Guard so he can help me carry your dead asses out of here 'cause I'm going to shoot you and your aide!"

The general slammed down the phone, shot an order to Captain Perfection who snapped to attention, after which they both stormed off down the corridor. You see, our positions had changed radically. Although I was far outranked, the General and his aide were outgunned. At that point I took over and I took the lead in this "chicken dance."

After a while, however, I began to wonder if I had totally screwed up. There was a nagging thought in the back of my mind that maybe the dance was not quite over. I was relieved at 0600 hours by the next shift, went to the mess hall for breakfast, showered and went to bed. About 1000 hours, the Charge of Quarters awakened me, told me to get dressed and report to Colonel Nice Guy's office ASAP. He also warned me that Colonel Nice Guy sounded unusually upset about something.

When I reported to the colonel's office, his administrative assistant, a sergeant buddy of mine, was shaking his head and asked what the hell kind of stunt I had pulled. Apparently the colonel had been on a tear after getting a phone call earlier in the morning, something that was totally out of character for him. I instantly had a vision of losing all of my stripes and getting to see the inside of a military prison after all. I was thinking that General SOB really must have peeled Colonel Nice Guy like an onion. I was convinced I was about to go through a similar process. I believed I had gone too far with General SOB and, as I was on the bottom rung of the chicken coop, everyone above me was going to dump all over me. It was one dance I very much did not want to attend.

After he let me sweat for about twenty minutes, I was ordered into Colonel Nice Guy's office where I stood ramrod straight at attention in front of his desk. The colonel glared at me from his seat of power behind his desk for what seemed like an hour. While I continued to stand at attention, eyes focused on the wall behind him, he told me that General SOB had told him, no had screamed at him, about an incident that happened about 0400 hours that morning. He described the incident involving General SOB, Captain Perfection and me (the sergeant) in detail just as it had occurred. He then asked me what the hell I said to the general when he threatened to force his way in behind the "steel door."

About that time, my knees were locking up, my brow was covered in perspiration, my throat was dry and I was getting concerned about my bladder. I knew that my career was over! I very quietly said, "Sir," I told the General I would "call the Corporal of the Guard."

With a deep furrow on his brow and a frustrated look on his face, he asked why I would say that. After swallowing hard and trying to clear my throat, I told him the same thing I told the general.

"That's the same story the general told me, so at least I know you're not lying about it," Colonel Nice Guy said. "Now tell me how the hell you came up with that answer."

My response was simple. Sir, I don't know. I knew his name wasn't on the list, he wasn't authorized behind the 'steel door' and I was going to shoot him!"

The Colonel told me to stand "at ease" at which point he broke into a broad grin totally confusing me. He said he had been in the military for about twenty-five years and that was one of the best stories he ever heard. He told me there were two reasons he called me into his office. First, he wanted to hear me tell the story. Second, he wanted to shake my hand and advise me that I had just passed a rigorous security test. General SOB was really a Master Sergeant and Captain Perfection was a Staff Sergeant, both of whom were assigned to a Military Police investigative unit from another base. The reason they had stormed off down the corridor was that they did not want me to see them laughing at my response. Apparently, they had been doing these checks for years and thought my response was at the top of their lifetime list of clever responses. Had I allowed them access, I probably would be writing a different book from some hole beneath the ground.

As it turned out, I finished my assignment about six weeks before I was supposed to be released from active duty. I remembered back to the first day I had discussed this assignment with Colonel Nice Guy. That is when he told me that when I took the assignment I would not be released until the assignment was completed. On that basis, I made an appointment to see Colonel Nice Guy, and a few days later found myself standing at attention in front of his desk, but without the dry mouth and sweaty armpits.

He asked me to state my business. In my mind it was very simple. If the order was that I couldn't be released from active duty until the assignment was completed, then why not release me early as the assignment had been completed early. After about two minutes of contemplation, Colonel Nice Guy guffawed. When he caught his breath, he said, "Sergeant, I have never met anyone like you. You are the most creative SOB I have ever met. I am going to cut your orders and send you home to get you the hell off the base before you give other troops any ideas."

If that weren't good enough, I got to fly home on December 31, 1959. That meant I got to celebrate the New Year in Japan and again in California, which to a twenty-one year old sergeant seemed like a dream. I was released from active duty a couple of days later, three weeks before my scheduled date. This only goes to prove one of my other beliefs. "If you don't ask, you don't get!"

This book is intended to give you a better perspective of what goes on during the "chicken dance" as well as providing you some insights and tools to enable you to progress through the various stages of building better relationships and alliances.

So what is the "chicken dance?" You've heard, and probably used, the expression "cock of the walk." That's nothing more than the head of the coop strutting around with their chest puffed out trying to attract the hens. You also have heard of the "pecking order." Put simply, that's nothing more than establishing who is sitting on the top shelf of the coop or the organization.

Among people, the chicken dance is the interaction that takes place throughout the day and throughout our lives. It goes on at the personal level as well as the professional level. If you are able to sit back and observe other people's behavior in the context of the "chicken dance," you will gain a better understanding of how people perceive themselves and their role in the task at hand. Throughout my professional career, I've observed something that goes on in all relationships, formal or informal. What goes on is a form of positioning for power and/or control, and as such it can take many forms.

As you read this chapter, you need to establish a mental image of the behavior of chickens in their environment and compare their behavior to your own experiences in the world. I would be willing to bet that by the end of this chapter, you will relate these actions and antics to recent events in your own life, and probably will be laughing at yourself when you have had time to think about it.

Put into perspective, many of our actions and antics are not very different from chickens in the barnyard and in the coop. The "chicken dance" is nothing more than the shuffle that chickens go through to position themselves in the hierarchy of the barnyard and the coop. Chickens run around squawking, clucking, flapping their wings, and pecking with no apparent direction. They preen themselves to gain recognition. Some assume an aggressive posture by puffing up their chests when another approaches their "perceived territory."

Human behavior does not deviate much from the antics of chickens. Try this experiment. Go into a bar some evening and observe the human preening, squawking and flapping taking place. It is the human equivalent of the "chicken dance" to gain position in a social setting. It is the dating, or mating, game in its simplest form which, in some cases, is the prelude to a longer term relationship or an alliance between two parties.

As an example, my wife and I were part of a group of seventeen families transferred to Mexico City by Ford Motor Company in 1974. While we were awaiting completion of our apartment, we stayed at the Maria Isabel Hotel, which was conveniently located right next door to the Ford offices. For a variety of reasons, we ended up staying in the hotel for four and a half months before moving into our apartment. One of the many bars and restaurants in the Maria Isabel, the Jorongo Bar, was popular with the tourists as it featured Mariachi music every evening. My wife and I enjoyed many hours there together. As I could speak Spanish, I quickly made friends with some of the staff and a group of seven Mexican bachelors who were obvious regulars at the bar. As it turned out these men became friends and truly added to the pleasure of our stay in Mexico over the next two and a half years.

Frequently, I would join the "group" for a drink after my wife and I had been out to dinner. In many cases my wife would excuse herself on the basis that it was late. The truth is that she got tired of listening to the Mariachi music night after night. She also got tired of watching our new found friends go through their version of the "chicken dance" night after night. Keep in mind most restaurants in Mexico City did not begin to serve dinner until 8:00 p.m., and in most cases, the only people showing up that early were the tourists.

The result was that I would end up socializing with my new found friends and watching them go through their version of the "chicken dance." I was convinced that this group rested up all day so they could devote their time—sometimes all night—to the conquest of American female tourists. Their dance was truly something to behold, and obviously had been practiced, rehearsed and polished over the years.

The bachelors would begin to drift in by themselves around 9:00 or 9:30 p.m. Upon arrival, each of them would work their way around the bar greeting friends and employees. This activity also provided them the opportunity to check out the crowd, and to see if there were any "newcomers." Eventually, the group would congregate just inside the entrance so they could check out all new arrivals. Once the "newcomers" had evaluated, the group would ensure they were noticed. By this time they would have had a few drinks, and they would begin to sing along with the Mariachis, naturally drawing attention in their direction. Any female tourist who happened to look their way and smile was now the focus of their attention, especially if she was with a group of other attractive female tourists.

Within minutes the women would find themselves with freshened drinks brought by one of the waiters, and soon would be joined by the "group." After exchanging names, whatever names the "group" decided was appropriate for that evening, the joking would begin. You need to understand that these Mexicans spoke English almost as well as they spoke Spanish, and they could carry on a conversation in either language. They also understood that their broken English, which Americans refer to as "Spanglish," appeared "cute" to the women. Once the introductions were complete, the "group" would seat themselves with the women. After much banter and laughter, as well as several more rounds of drinks, the guys would teach the women the words to one or two of the more popular songs being sung by a very loud Mariachi band. Sometimes they would join the ladies on stage to sing with the Mariachi band. Of course, the women would be impressed, but did not realize that the band was an integral part of the "chicken dance." In other words, it all was prearranged.

Sometimes, the "group" would depart for dinner with all the women, and sometimes the "group" would drift off somewhere else only to pick up where they left off the next evening. While I did not keep score, I would have to give the "group" an 80 to 90% success rating. Intuitively the "group" had polished the steps of the "chicken dance" to the point where it was totally natural to them. It no longer was a ritual, but part of their everyday life, which they looked forward to with great anticipation. It appeared that it was the challenge as much as the conquest that kept them coming back every night.

I happened to return to Mexico City several years later on business. I could hardly wait until I completed my meetings the first day to return to the Jorongo Bar and see what was taking place. I was not disappointed. I was delighted to find five members of the original seven still in action. Only the tourists had changed. The "chicken dance" was still going on, and it still appeared to be successful!

In the business arena, the dance takes many forms. It can be seen in a meeting where the person in charge seats themselves at the head of the table — the position of power. Think about the last time you were invited or summoned to someone else's office. If they remained behind their desk, and you were seated on the opposite side, that is an affirmation of the office holder's power.

Early in my career at Ford, I was called into a vice president's office to answer questions about a presentation I had made earlier in the day. This gentleman was no more than five feet tall (shorter than I am) when I had last seen him, but when I was sitting in front of his desk, he towered over me. I found out later that he had his office chairs constructed to raise his position behind the desk while slightly shortening the visitors' chair legs so he could command from his position. I did not think about it at the time, but he may have taken his cue from the courtroom structure where the judge sits above the other participants. It certainly adds to the aura of power.

Next time you attend a meeting, try the following exercise in organizational behavior. Before you do so, however, remember that laughing to yourself is okay, while laughing out loud could get you ejected from the meeting. Worse yet, it may even get you ejected from the company.

First, observe the other people in the room. Who has taken the seat at the head of the table suggesting that "I am in charge." Who is attempting to gain position through frequent and sometimes unnecessary challenges to the person presenting? Could this be a form of puffing the chest? Who continuously restates some points already made to demonstrate their knowledge? Who brings the greatest number of unrelated props to bolster their rank like the new leather briefcase, a gold pen, or some other prop? Is this not like preening? All of these antics are nothing more than the "chicken dance" in action in a business environment.

In a business environment, these antics take many forms and can be observed through:

- Attire
- Verbiage
- Seating position
- Props
- Demeanor
- Physical location and positioning

Initial Steps

They have worked for years, and I can vouch for every one of them. I know they work because at one time or another I have used them.

Props, of course, can take any form contingent upon the particular situation. While in the midst of negotiating a technology licensing agreement with Suiryo Plastics Co., Ltd., a well-recognized Japanese automotive supplier of vehicle interiors, we became stuck on a key point in the contract, resulting in a delay in getting the agreement signed. As a result, the negotiations had stretched out over a period of about eight months. Part of the problem was that Mr. "O," the gentleman with whom I was negotiating, was the Vice President of Technology for Suiryo, and was constantly traveling throughout Europe and Asia on other business matters. I also was involved in several other deals and was traveling extensively.

The good news was that because of the protracted negotiations, Mr. "O" and I had become friends. The friendship has lasted more than twenty-five years, long beyond the time we both retired from our respective companies.

The general manager of the automotive supplier company that I was representing in the negotiations was impatient to get the technology. His expectations were not very realistic or reasonable. I therefore dubbed him "Mr. Unreasonable." Mr. Unreasonable quickly got nervous about how long the negotiations were lasting and began to believe I would be unable to successfully finish the agreement. At the same time, he had established the "bottom line" on an extremely sticky negotiating point and was unwilling to move from his position.

"If you can't get the contract signed," he warned, "I will find someone else who can do your job. You have one more chance to wrap this up!"

Not exactly what I wanted to hear especially because arbitrary deadlines tend to result in less than optimum agreements. Mr. Unreasonable had put me in the position of having one hand tied behind my back while trying to buy technology from a well respected Japanese automotive supplier company. He also had applied additional pressure by establishing an arbitrary deadline. As he had given me an ultimatum, the situation called for something unique to get the other party to move on a key point in the negotiations. I felt as though I may have run out of alternatives.

About that time, I received a call from Mr. "O," who was in Switzerland on business. He said he would be available to meet with me in London in about a week to hopefully conclude our negotiations. As traveling to London was a lot easier on my body and easier on the company's wallet than traveling to Japan, I made all the arrangements. What a perfect opportunity to set the stage for something creative. Now all I had to do was come up with something.

Mr. "O" arrived in London at roughly the same time I did, and after settling into the hotel, we spent a couple of hours socializing in the lobby coffee bar. We then went out for a relaxing dinner, accompanied by a bottle of wine and some interesting conversation about world events. Neither of us mentioned the business at hand. Providing time for social interaction without discussing business is an essential element of relationships, even more so in some cultures.

After breakfast the next morning, we went to our meeting location. Fortunately for me, it was a private and exclusive home provided by the company I was representing. The dining room had been converted to a meeting room that would serve as the setting for the Board of Directors for any large company. The dining room table could have seated at least 30 people. In addition, there was a full staff on duty to address any needs we might have, including preparing and serving lunch and dinner as necessary.

I was somewhat taken aback by the luxury of the surroundings and the formality of the staff. The butler, the chef and the wait staff, all greeted us upon our arrival. If that were not enough of an impression, they all were dressed in formal attire. We continued on to a meeting room where we would try to find a way to finish the agreement. After almost four hours of discussion, it appeared that we were still at "square one" and might not be able to accomplish our objective. This outcome would have been disastrous for me given Mr. Unreasonable's directions to me.

At that point, I excused myself and advised Mr. "O" that I was going to make luncheon arrangements. I advised the chef and the head waiter that I would like to use the formal dining room for lunch, which appeared a bit unusual to them. I explained that Mr. "O" and I were far apart in our negotiations and that I wanted to use the dining room to make the point even more obvious than it already was. Accordingly, I asked them to seat Mr. "O" at one end of the table and to seat me at the extreme opposite end. When we entered the dining room and Mr. "O" was seated, he looked at me across a distance of about thirty feet with a very puzzled look on his face. I said nothing, but spent a minute or so getting settled at my end of the table.

When he could no longer contain himself, Mr. "O" very quietly inquired if other people were joining us for lunch or if I was upset about something and didn not want to sit together during our luncheon. Bingo, I thought. Mr. "O" is concerned about the relationship. Now I knew the relationship was as meaningful to him as it was to me. My response was simple. With a smile on my face, I told him the place settings were arranged the way they were to demonstrate to him how far apart we still were in our negotiations after all of this time and energy. I told him I was hoping we could continue to discuss the one remaining point while we had lunch, and "maybe by the end of it we would be sitting side by side on the same side of the table."

After a good laugh, we continued our business discussion. Just to use the prop to its fullest extent, each time we circled around the one remaining negotiating point and got a bit closer, I moved my chair closer to Mr. "O." This approach seemed to work as we had many laughs, and by the end of the day we were sitting side by side, putting our heads together and drafting the final language.

The dining room prop appeared to be the icebreaker. I was out of options and effectively found myself between the proverbial "rock and a hard place." Mr. "O" probably sensed that I was being boxed in by a higher authority, but could not be certain. Fortunately, the license turned out to be excellent for both parties. For me, the good news was that I had made another friend even though the negotiations were very difficult at times.

Just as a footnote, many years later I was back in Japan trying to negotiate another license agreement between two different parties. I was having a great deal of difficulty reaching agreement with Sumitomo Chemical Company, which held a patent on the technology my client wanted. I took a day away from the negotiating table to spend with my friend Mr. "O." To my surprise and delight, Mr. "O" knew a lot about the other company. He also knew some of the people from Sumitomo who were at the negotiating table. After providing me with as much information as he could, Mr. "O" had only one question. He looked me in the eye and with a straight face asked if I was going to "treat them to a luncheon in London or was that only for me?"

"No, Mr. 'O,' I said, "I only host luncheons like that for very special friends." We shared another good laugh, shook hands, bowed to one another and promised to stay in touch, which we do to this day.

When taken to the next level, where two teams from different business disciplines, corporate cultures or ethnic cultures get together to assess working together, the fun really begins. Cultural differences sometimes add another level of complexity to the "chicken dance." An even broader set of interactions takes place when two teams come together to try to determine the potential for an ongoing relationship. Team members of the respective teams will tend to align themselves according to rank and perceived power. Other team members will tend to gravitate toward those from the same or similar business discipline to attain a certain comfort level.

What is even more interesting is to observe the actions and antics of the teams as they posture to demonstrate who has the stronger hand in the early stages of the discussion. Noting the antics of the various members of both teams is an excellent way to gain insights into other's personal and business priorities and needs. These insights should become the cornerstone of your understanding of the other participants. You need to remember that these are the people who will play a key role in your discussions should they progress to the next stage.

As team leader in several alliance discussions, I was responsible for: establishing and building the team, the agenda for the discussions, communication with key internal stakeholders, location for the discussions, venues for social activities such as dinners, seating arrangements at the meetings and many other details. As such, I also had to ensure that our team members represented the various business disciplines involved in the forthcoming discussions.

The social interaction between and among team members is critical to set the stage for discussions with the other party. One of the worst things that can occur is to have one of your team members commit a "faux pas," or unwittingly insult a member of the other team during the early stages of the encounter. This occurrence could cause you to have to rebuild relationships before you ever start the actual discussions. Worse yet is not being aware that a "faux pas" has occurred and going on as though nothing has happened. For example, in some countries crossing your legs and exposing the sole of your shoe to the other party is considered an insult. Unfortunately, there is no magic formula to ensure that you and your team will never commit a social blunder or inadvertently insult the other party due to cultural differences. Before the first meeting, to reduce the likelihood of these negative events from occurring, team members should be thoroughly briefed and prepared in several areas.

On one occasion, I was doing business in China with a team of people who had never worked together. I had been hired by a joint venture company, with each partner assigning two people to the team. As a result, the team was composed of a retired Canadian toolmaker, a Chinese businessperson who had worked briefly for an automotive company in Brazil and who now lived in Brazil, a young engineer and a young financial analyst, neither of whom had ever been outside the US. What a strange sight we must have been traveling around China together.

At our first meeting we focused on the task ahead as well as the complexities of trying to form a joint venture with a Chinese company while trying to satisfy the needs of the two parties to the joint venture we were representing. To say that this project was doomed from the start would be polite. I do not believe that three-party alliances have good long term prospects. Trying to build a successful alliance in China in the mid 1990s when a market oriented industry was not fully understood and doing so with an inexperienced team added another layer of complexity.

In any event, we finished our briefings and began our odyssey through seven cities in China speaking with government officials at each location. In each city we were entertained by our hosts at dinner. The Chinese are gracious hosts and there are protocols that are expected to be followed at these dinners. For example, there are toasts and welcoming speeches to be made before dining. One of the key cultural mores about which the team was briefed was that there was to be no fraternization with members of the opposite sex while we were guests there.

The team was advised that, if anyone was perceived as having an inappropriate relationship with a member of the opposite sex, their passport would be stamped "persona non grata" and they would be sent out of the country. Unfortunately, after partying with our hosts after dinner one evening, our young engineer danced one waltz (a favorite pastime of the Chinese) with a female engineer from the Chinese government team. The next day the female engineer was conspicuously absent from the discussions. Worse yet, I was called aside and it was suggested that one of our team members be replaced. While we completed this round of the discussions, our engineer was kept away from the main table. He stayed at the hotel working on reports, and was reassigned upon our return to the US.

This situation again reinforced the importance of fully briefing team members before the first meeting on the following key items:

- The purpose of the discussions
- Team objectives
- Corporate/senior management politics
- A profile of the other company's business
- Profiles of the other party's team members
- Appropriate topics for discussion and agendas for each meeting
- Topics to be avoided
- Inappropriate behavior

Initial Steps

The interplay between the parties is vital to the relationship. It is the first step in any relationship, and until this unstructured "chicken dance" takes place, it will be impossible for the discussions to move forward.

I certainly do not know when the first chicken dance took place. The following excerpt from Cullen Murphy's book *Are We Rome?* suggests that it has been going on for a long time and that it serves its purpose. In a chapter entitled "When Power Meets Reality," Mr. Murphy states, "Both Rome and America, again at their most adroit, benefit from the psychological impact of military strength; how the mere perception of power begets additional power, and makes unnecessary the actual use of force. In 1995, at an air base in Ohio, as belligerents from the Balkans argued stubbornly over the details of the Dayton Accords, American negotiators fostered the cooperation of the Serbian leader, Slobodan Milosevic, by seating him directly under a cruise missile. Once to encourage a spirit of mature reflection among a delegation of barbarians, the emperor Hadrian ordered a unit of mounted cavalry — in full armor, in perfect formation — to swim across the Danube and back. The barbarians, writes Cassius Dio, 'stood in terror of the Romans' and turning their attention to their own affairs, they employed Hadrian as an arbitrator of their differences.' (Pages 71-72). These examples, though centuries apart, clearly demonstrate the benefits of understanding the "chicken dance" and the positioning and power that can result when the dance steps are well executed.

You probably recognize that you already have been to the dance many times and that in most cases you have gotten caught up in the rhythm without knowing the dance steps. Having a clearer mental image of the steps employed by others, and preparing your team to dance in step with one another should help you get *Beyond the Chicken Dance*.

Before moving on there are a four stories I want to share with you that will help reinforce just how the "chicken dance" can take place. As I said before, you just need to be aware of what is taking place so you are not unknowingly disadvantaged.

CHICKEN DANCE MEETS MEXICAN HAT DANCE

It seems as though no matter how long I recognized the fact that the "chicken dance" always preceded negotiations, I always was learning new steps to the dance routine. Even though the ultimate objective of the dance – to gain power or position – never changes, adding the element of a new culture to the mix, always brings additional, and somewhat different, steps to the dance routine.

In the situation that follows, the "chicken dance" dragged out over a period of years, and ultimately, crossed the border into Mexico where it became commingled with some steps from the "Mexican Hat Dance" – an interesting combination to say the least!

Just to set the stage, I had been working for Ford in Mexico during the period 1974 - 1977. In early 1980, I was the business planning manager for one of Ford's component manufacturing divisions in Michigan. Back then all the division's manufacturing operations were located in Southeast Michigan.

To the extent the division required additional manufacturing capacity, I believed that they should seriously consider establishing operations in Mexico. There were significant advantages to locate there to access lower labor costs, government incentives, as well as export credits, just to name a few.

To me, it seemed like a "no brainer," and I convinced myself that everyone would sign up to be on the team to develop the project. Accordingly, I set up a meeting with the general manager and a few department heads, and invited them to a presentation outlining the benefits of locating in Mexico versus building new facilities in the same area of Michigan. I was so sure of myself that I wanted all the "top dogs" in the division to be there to participate. The meeting was attended by the general manager, "Gregarious Bob," who of course was positioned at the head of the table. Gregarious Bob was flanked by his controller, and his director of operations. Also seated along both sides of the table were the director of human resources, all four local plant managers, and just about every other manager who caught wind of the meeting. I, of course was seated at the far end of the table, opposite Gregarious Bob.

As I looked around the room, it was a full house and I was about to lead what I believed was a well orchestrated dance. I must admit that in retrospect, it felt as though the whole world was looking down at me.

Well, I outlined the proposal to Gregarious Bob who very quickly told me that I must be out of my mind. He vigorously advised me that he believed Southeast Michigan was the right location, and he would never consider operating or living outside the US. As he is saying the words, he is flushing from red to purple, and the veins in his neck appeared ready to explode. It was about that time that the dance routine changed radically. Every one of the department heads and managers either leaned back away from the table or physically pushed their chairs back from the table. Other than the shift in position sending a clear signal that I had absolutely no support, it also gave Gregarious Bob a much clearer shot at me!

Of course, everyone else in the room remained mute for a moment, after which a few of my "close allies" started taking "pot shots" at the assumptions in the study. Once on a roll, of course, they continued to attack the conclusion and the recommendation. After all, why jump in on the dance floor when the music is off key.

The funny part is about six months later Gregarious Bob accepted a job in Brazil where he remained for several years. After that he spent many years in Europe running other operations for Ford before returning to the US. So much for not getting involved in operations outside the US or living abroad.

Once the new general manager settled in, I blew the dust off my "Mexican Proposal," rescued it from my desk drawer and gave it another shot. This time, to my surprise, I was encouraged to continue. Back then Mexican law required that automotive suppliers be established as joint ventures with the local partner owning a majority interest. That began the next phase of the "chicken dance," and I did not have a clue as to just how many new dance steps I was about to learn.

Once we selected a partner, from several candidates, it took six months of continuous negotiations to "ink the deal." To say that the negotiations were interesting and educational would be an understatement, particularly as this was my first endeavor in negotiating a joint venture between two very large business entities both of which had a very definitive list of "must haves."

Once signed, the next phase of the "chicken dance/ Mexican hat dance" began. As the facility was constructed and the workforce trained, new steps were being introduced every month. It seemed as though the two parties were continuously jockeying for position.

Although the initial phase followed a bumpy path, the parties had the foresight to look at the long term benefits and work out their differences. Once the manufacturing operation was "up and running," and was producing adequate quantities of high quality parts, both parties got "beyond the chicken dance." At that point, they sat around the table rather than opposite one another and put their heads together to "make the pie bigger." At the end of the day, they each ended up with a bigger piece of pie.

CHICKEN DANCE, CHICKEN RANCH OR MUSTANG RANCH?

About thirteen years ago while most of us were focused on preparing for the impact of Y2000, an event that was again overplayed in the media, there were other significant events taking place in the world. Among other key events, the EURO currency was first introduced, there was a war going on in Kosovo, Hugo Chavez was elected President of Venezuela, Putin replaced Yeltsin as President of Russia, and Bill Clinton was acquitted by the Senate in his impeachment.

Something else was taking place that most of us never heard about. Looking back at what transpired, and the result, makes me think that having the Federal Government involved in business might not be the best alternative. If history repeats itself, it may be the least desirable alternative.

Here's what happened. As a result of losing a federal case for racketeering and fraud in 1999, the Mustang Ranch, a legal brothel near Reno, Nevada, was forfeited to the Federal Government. The Mustang Ranch was the first brothel in Nevada to be licensed. It was by far the biggest legal brothel as measured by annual revenue. Its revenues reportedly were greater than the combined revenues of all the other legal brothels in Nevada. In 2002, a mere three years later, the assets of the Mustang Ranch including its paintings, its furniture, its accessories, etc., were auctioned off by the federal government. The bar stools, the beds and bedding, the bidets and the room numbers were auctioned off in an attempt to recover the former owner's back taxes. Ultimately, the government got creative and put the Mustang Ranch up for bid on eBay where it sold for the grand sum of $145,100. It has since been reopened by the successful bidder.

The point here is that if the Federal Government could not make a go of a legal business entity whose principal products were prostitution and liquor, what was their real motive for getting into the banking, automotive and health care industries? It certainly cannot be profit motivated! Are we now looking at using our taxpayer dollars on a continuing basis to provide ongoing bailouts to industries where the federal government has increased their involvement and gained more control? Is this the beginning of another giant chicken dance, where we the taxpayers are being dragged to the dance floor involuntarily, or is it something more in line with what used to go on at the Mustang Ranch?

From where I sit, the conclusion is obvious. If you cannot make money at the oldest profession in the world, you have no business running any other enterprise! Guess we'll just have to wait and see.

✻ ✻ ✻

THE ULTIMATE CHICKEN DANCE

You have taken part in it. You may even have initiated it. The fact is, it goes on at all levels and in all situations, both personal and business.

Now that you recognize the "chicken dance" for what it is, this story should serve to reinforce in your mind that it precedes all negotiations irrespective of the stakes. It stems from the perception in someone's mind that they can gain position against the other party before even entering into the matter at hand.

The following story shows how the steps to the "chicken dance" were orchestrated over a period of years through a series of legal gyrations.

During the early 1980s a friend of mine, Mike, who was a young aspiring lawyer in Michigan, was appointed to represent an indigent defendant in an appeal of his conviction. Back then, the Supreme Court had decided that any indigent defendant was entitled to a free transcript of his trial for use on appeal. To clarify, **the defendant was entitled to a free copy of the entire trial transcript.**

The trial judge would not order a copy of the entire trial transcript for use by Mike so he could effectively represent the defendant on appeal. Instead the judge ordered Mike to talk to the attorney who originally tried the case. Not surprisingly, but unfortunately, the attorney could not remember which issues arose during the trial.

Now Mike had to return to the judge and again request the entire trial transcript, an uncomfortable situation at best. Instead of complying with the Supreme Court decision, the judge ordered only select portions of the transcript relating to pretrial issues. I can just imagine the level of frustration that Mike was experiencing. To add to Mike's level of frustration, the judge let it be known he was taking this approach to save time and taxpayer money. Yah, right your honor! (that's my opinion). Let's see how much we saved at the end of the day.

The next step was to appeal the case in the US Court of Appeals for the Sixth District. Now here is where the fun, or frustration, really intensified. During oral argument, the government attorney had no response whatsoever to Mike's argument. One would think that the case would be over at this point. Not really! The Court of Appeals upheld the trial court's earlier decision. As a result, Mike took the only remaining step and appealed the case to the Supreme Court, the most powerful court in the US. On the basis that both the trial court and the appellate court chose to ignore the clear ruling from the Supreme Court regarding the trial transcript, the Supreme Court agreed to hear the case.

Mike was overjoyed at the thought of having the opportunity to argue a case in front of the Supreme Court. Shortly after reviewing the case, the Solicitor General for the US filed a brief in agreement with Mike's argument, and the Supreme Court issued an order reversing the lower court's decision. As a result, there was no need for oral argument in front of the Supreme Court, so Mike never got his 30 minutes of fame.

This process took roughly 1 1/2 years just to get Mike an obvious and just decision. Now the case had to go back to the trial court which then ordered what he was entitled to get from the beginning. How much do you suppose this saved the taxpayers, your honor?

After that, Mike had to file a new brief before the US Court of Appeals incorporating any issues discovered in the remainder of the transcript. The findings confirmed the defendant's conviction.

We'll never know if the defendant's sentence could have been overturned faster than the three years it took to get through the court system "chicken dance." My best guess is that had Mike been given the entire trial transcript he originally requested, the Court of Appeals may have sided with Mike the first time around. Two results would have occurred under this scenario. First, much time and effort could have been saved. As it turned out, the appeal process took longer than the defendant's original sentence. Furthermore, the cost to the taxpayers would have been significantly less without all the gyrations of not complying with the Supreme Court's direction to begin with.

So, here is further proof that purely positioning for power or employing the "chicken dance" to gain something of perceived value from someone else, usually results in less than an optimum outcome. Unfortunately, it still goes on all the time!

HOW THE CHICKEN GOT TO THE DINING TABLE

Recently, while waiting in a doctor's office, I happened to pick up a copy of the June, 2013 edition of the *Smithsonian* magazine. By chance the magazine contained an article entitled "How the Chicken Conquered the World" by Jerry Alder and Andrew Lawler, which I thought would be a great way to conclude this chapter.

"The chickens that saved Western Civilization were discovered, according to legend, by the side of the road in Greece in the first decade of the fifth century B.C. The Athenian general Themistocles, on his way to confront the invading Persian forces, stopped to watch two cocks fighting and summoned his troops, saying 'Behold, these do not fight for their household gods, for the monuments of their ancestors, for glory, for liberty or the safety of their children, but only because one will not give way to the other.' The tale does not describe what happened to the loser, nor explain why the soldiers found this display of instinctive aggression inspirational rather than pointless and depressing. But history records that the Greeks, thus heartened, went on to repel the invaders, preserving the civilization that today honors those same creatures by breeding, frying, and dipping them into one's choice of sauce. The descendants of those roosters might well think – if they were capable of such profound thought – that their ancient forbears have a lot to answer for."

..... "In, *Guns, Germs and Steel,* Jared Diamond listed chickens among the 'small domestic mammals and domestic birds and insects' that have been useful to humanity but unlike the horse or the ox did little – outside of legends – to change the course of history. Nonetheless, the chicken has inspired contributions to culture, art, cuisine, science and religion over the millenia. Chickens were, and still are, a sacred animal in some cultures. The prodigious and ever-watchful hen was a worldwide symbol of nurturance and fertility. Eggs hung in Egyptian temples to ensure a bountiful river flood. The lusty rooster (a.k.a. cock) was a universal signifier of virility – but also, in the ancient Persian faith of Zoroastrianism, a benign spirit that crowed at dawn to herald a turning point in the cosmic struggle between darkness and light. For the Romans, the chicken's killer app was fortunetelling, especially during wartime. Chickens accompanied Roman armies, and their behavior was carefully observed before battle; a good appetite meant victory was likely.........."

The story goes on and there are many more interesting tales about chickens. The point is, that the chicken dance takes many forms and there a many conclusions you can draw from the history of chickens.

Simply put, your takeaway from this chapter should be that understanding what goes on when you are involved in the chicken dance will help you continue on more solid footing as you enter the next stage of building relationships.

CHAPTER 3

CULTURAL SNAPSHOTS

If you were starting to breed chickens, you certainly would want to know about the different breeds, their characteristics and how they behave. You certainly would not consider putting two different breeds in the same flock without first knowing something about the possibilities of their getting along and improving your chances of success. Because people behave a lot like chickens, if you are considering entering into a relationship or an alliance, it makes sense to understand the background and nature of your potential partner before entering into a long term relationship. I am sure that you are aware of many times when this has not been the case. As a result, the parties tend to get frustrated and wind up wasting time and energy. Also negotiations tend to get more complicated than necessary, and in the worst case, the relationship breaks down completely.

By understanding the differences between yourself and the other party's culture, you will be establishing a more solid foundation from which to continue. This understanding becomes even more relevant as many of the decisions we make have international implications.

Let's look at some of the chicken breeds and their behavioral characteristics as set forth in Henderson's Chicken Breed Chart from the Mad City web site. This chart provides a variety of details on more than 60 chicken breeds, and would appear to be very useful if you were considering starting a flock. Other information on selected breeds (e.g. Rijnlander & Sulmtaler) came from different web sites from around the world, in particular, www.kippengrabbelton.be from Belgium.

You can draw your own conclusions, but it seems to me that not only do chickens and humans share some traits, but some breeds appear to reflect perceived characteristics of their native culture.

Cultural Snapshots

The IC You See Handy-Dandy Chicken Chart*

Breed	Type	Origin	Behavior
Ameraucana	Layer	South America	Mostly calm, non-aggressive
Ancona	Layer	Italy	Active, flighty, marked wildness
Barnevelder	Dual Purpose	Holland	Active, hens friendly; cocks Aggressive
Buttercup	Layer	Sicily	Very fidgety, active, flighty, wild
Chabo	True Bantam	Japan	Generally friendly; cocks can be aggressive

New Hampshire & Rhode Island Reds	Dual Purpose	U.S.	Can be friendly or aggressive
Dorking	Dual Purpose	England	Calm, stately, gentle, friendly
Rijlander	Layer	Germany	Very tough, confident temperament
Sulmtaler	Dual Purpose	Germany	Calm, square and tough
Wyandotte	Dual Purpose	U.S.	Calm, industrious, normally docile, but can turn aggressive; some friendly, some aloof

*Henderson's Chicken Breed Chart, *www.madcitychickens.com*

By now you should be getting the picture that chicken breeds are targeted for specific purposes, and that each breed has distinct, defining characteristics. It is also interesting to see that chickens and people share some common characteristics.

About 25 years ago, I participated in the successful acquisition of the Parker Chemical Division of Occidental Petroleum. Parker already had a broad international presence. As it turned out, Parker also had a complex network of technology licensing and cross-licensing agreements covering a vast geographic area on several continents. These licensing agreements provided that any time the company changed ownership, all licensing agreements were open for renegotiation. As a result, the President of Parker Chemical, and its new owner Ford Motor Company, requested that I assist in resolving the disputes that had arisen among some European licensees. One case in particular stands out.

The German licensee had been unable to resolve differences with an Italian sublicensee. Both of these companies were using chemical formulations from Parker Chemical, as well as some of their own to manufacture metal pretreatment products.

It appeared to me that their cultural differences were making it difficult for them to agree. Look at the preceding chart on chicken breeds paying particular attention to characteristics of the Ancona (Italy) and Buttercup (Sicily) in contrast to the Rijnlander (Germany) and the Sulmtaler (Germany). The differences between the two parties at the negotiating table were similar to the characteristics of these chicken breeds.

To further complicate matters, the Italian team was represented by identical twin brothers who always seemed to be out of sync with one another. At first, it appeared they might be playing the Italian version of "Good Cop, Bad Cop," but as it turned out, their emotions just happened to be triggered at different times, and for different reasons. In contrast, from all outward appearances the German team members were calm and cohesive. In reality, however, they were containing themselves in appearance only and were on the verge of exploding and walking away from the negotiations. Had the parties "agreed to disagree," some long-standing relationships as well as business would have been terminated. Ford, the new owner, would have lost significant value in the newly acquired business due to reduced European sales and lower technology licensing fees.

In an attempt to save these relationships and the related business, I stole a strategy from Dr. Henry Kissinger and followed his approach of "shuttle diplomacy." Essentially, I sat with each "offended" party on their turf and set out to accomplish two objectives — first to let each party vent about the other, and second, to identify the real contractual issues. For example, the German team members were not comfortable with the emotional swings between the Italian brothers. They needed someone to intervene and get the negotiations done in a more orderly manner. Just as important to them was the ability to express their frustration with the proceedings to date. Once done, it was fairly easy to defuse the situation, bring the parties to their senses and finish a contract that worked for everyone, including the new owners of the company.

Obviously all negotiations are unique for the people involved and the issues to be addressed. There are, however, some fundamentals that need to be understood by all involved parties. The next chapter is intended to strengthen your understanding of the negotiating process and provide you with tips that should lead you to a more satisfactory negotiating experience.

CHAPTER 4

EVERYTHING IN LIFE IS NEGOTIABLE

Of all aspects of building better relationships and alliances, many of the people who I know find the process of negotiation to be difficult and uncomfortable. Most of these people have admitted to me that given the choice, they would prefer not to participate in negotiations.

I have to admit that for me the process of negotiating is fun and it is rewarding. One of the reasons I enjoy it is there are no fixed rules. There are unlimited possibilities. It is where creativity comes into play.

What appears to be so ominous to many people is something they probably do not realize is part of their everyday life. Every day we are surrounded by opportunities to negotiate. Whether you realize it or not, you are negotiating all day every day both at work and at home. Think about a typical day in your life. You probably have negotiated with a customer, a supplier or another employee. Then you go home and negotiate with your spouse and your children. Children are very smart. They just keep asking for something until they get what they want. Negotiating never ends, so why not improve your skills.

Again, I want to emphasize that whether you are aware of it, in some way you are negotiating every day of your life. If you own a dog, or have seen a friend or neighbor with their dog, I am sure you already are aware of how often negotiations come into play during the daily interaction between the dog and **their** people.

I can relate to "dog negotiations" as I have the good fortune to continue to learn from my pal Hooch, the West Highland Terrier, who is in the photo on the back cover. Hooch has helped me refine my negotiating skills by demonstrating to me that terriers can be very independent and "plant their feet in cement" when they make up their mind to do so. They really are not much different from some people with whom we find ourselves negotiating. They may listen, but they do not hear what is being offered, and there is a monumental difference between listening and hearing what is being said.

Hooch and I spend a lot time on the beach so he can explore, chase crabs, chase birds, swim and "meet and greet" all of his canine and human friends. He has become so well known that some people go out of their way to look for him during their beach outings.

When people first meet us, they often comment on how well behaved Hooch is. I often have heard, "I am amazed at how well behaved that dog is. He'll do anything you tell him to do." My response always is the same. "Yes, he really is outstanding. He will do anything I ask, as long as he agrees!"

The reality is that Hooch and I have reached a mutually satisfactory understanding over the years through a series of negotiations and compromise. Now we have a great relationship that is obvious to everyone who knows us. I just hope it goes on for a lot more years.

So, the real question is, how can you become a more skillful and a more successful negotiator? What tips can be learned to achieve more satisfactory and longer lasting results so that you do not have to confront the same hurdles repeatedly just hoping for a better result?

Well, to begin with you need to understand some of the fundamentals. The starting point is your own approach to negotiations. If you view negotiations as "win-lose" transactions, they may feel good to you in the short term if you are the "winner," but over time reality will set in that the outcome was unbalanced, and not necessarily fair to the other party. You will soon come to the realization that the other party was not satisfied and will continue to negotiate with you to gain back what they think they have lost. If you do not believe it, just think about bedtime negotiations with your children. How often do they try to gain additional leeway? How about the last time there was a decision to be made about which movie to see? Still cannot relate? Think about the last time you tried to get your pet to do what you wanted. How many tries did that take before your pet agreed or you just gave up?

The key to any successful negotiation is that each party recognizes they have to make concessions and they have gained some concessions from the other party. In other words, at the end of the day both parties should feel as though they have "won."

While I stand firm in my conviction that "everything in life is negotiable," I must admit that there are situations where direct negotiations are not viable or effective. If you have been in the military or know anything at all about life in the military, you know exactly where I'm headed. For example, the drill instructor says that everyone will "fall out at 0500 hours." That means, without exception, everyone will be awake, cleaned up, dressed and ready to go at five a.m. You do not get to negotiate whether you can make up your bed afterwards or shower and shave when you return. It means you will do what you are told without asking why and without trying to modify the conditions in any way.

Military life and the rules that govern it are different by necessity. Picture military life where there is an opportunity for the troops to question the orders of the First Sergeant, or their Commanding Officer. Here's the scenario. The troops are on a scouting mission in enemy territory. They are in single file, spread out along both sides of the road watching out for enemy snipers, etc. All of a sudden the Commanding Officer shouts "get down!" Normal training would ensure that every person on the team got down and sought protective cover. If, however, there was even a remote possibility to "negotiate," the troops would be standing around talking about things like: finding better cover, looking for softer or drier ground, whether it should be the left or the right side of the road, taking a smoke break first, or anything else they might want to challenge. My best guess is everyone except the Commanding Officer would be dead before the questions were answered. The Commanding Officer would still be alive because he would have found cover as he was shouting the command to "get down!"

As I said earlier, there are exceptions to the rule. I hope that when you find yourself in the middle of a negotiation, you will not hear the words "get down" coming from someone in the room. Having recognized that, wouldn't it be helpful to better understand some of the common pitfalls associated with negotiations, to gain a comfort level with the process and to get insights on how to develop techniques to achieve better outcomes for everyone involved? By the time you have absorbed the content of this chapter, you already should feel more comfortable with negotiations and should be looking forward to achieving a better outcome at your next negotiation.

Chances are that you and most people you know are uncomfortable with "formal" negotiations for several reasons. First, you do not believe that negotiating is a natural event. Formal negotiations tend to be viewed from the perspective that the only possible outcome from a negotiation is that one party "wins" and the other party "loses." Unfortunately, that is the approach that many people take when negotiating. Even more unfortunately, that approach does not lead to a good long term outcome as the final agreement will be unbalanced and unfair.

Think about how often you've walked into a store, picked out an item, gone to the checkout counter and paid the price shown on the ticket. Not every time, but in many instances you have left something on the table. Had you negotiated, you really could have done better. Just because there is a price tag on an item does not mean that you have to accept it. You are probably shaking your head and saying, "Yeah right, I'll just walk in to a store and tell the sales person that their price is too high and I want a lower price!"

Before you laugh too hard, next time you go into a store, keep the following points in mind:

- You are the customer
- The sales person wants to make a sale
- Your money will spend anywhere
- There are competitors' stores offering the same merchandise
- You need to be convinced why you should buy the item from the store you are in, as opposed to somewhere else

If the salesperson, and perhaps even the store manager, do not understand the situation from your perspective, they need to be made aware of your thought process in a gentle way. In other words, you need to get them to understand that if they do not in some way satisfy you, you probably will take your money somewhere else to get a better deal. You really do not have to hit them over the head with a hammer to get them to understand that you are the customer, and that the potential for making — or losing — the sale is in their hands.

When my wife goes shopping for something she looks forward to the challenge of negotiating a better deal. As an example, when she finds an article of clothing she wants to buy at a local store, she'll raise several challenging points with the sales person including the following:

- When is your next sale?
- How soon will this item be going on sale?
- It seems to me that XYZ store just announced a sale on a similar item. Maybe I should go there and see if this item is included.
- You know, I really like doing business with you and your store. Is there anything you can do to help me out?
- I don't want to put you in the middle so why don't we talk to the store manager and see if they can help.

Try these simple steps and watch what happens. It will not always work, and it may require that the store manager get involved, but you'll be pleasantly surprised by how often you will save money. You also will be amazed when you tell the story, how much fun you had in the process.

This approach also applies to higher-priced, "big ticket" items. To reinforce the point, the last three new home purchases we made all resulted in significant savings even though we were emphatically told by the senior sales representative that "the developer will not negotiate price." The price may have been fixed, but the developers in the first two instances were willing to include significant extras at no additional cost. This way the developer could remain steadfast in his position not to "negotiate price," and at the same time, satisfy our desire to improve the value of the deal for ourselves. The outcome was that all parties were satisfied. The developer sold a unit, the sales person received a commission and we felt we had obtained value for the price paid.

In the third instance, the VP of Sales lectured me for 30 minutes not to attempt to negotiate price with the developer, as though to do so would be an insult. While we were driving to the developer's office I was thinking about how much fun it was going to be to get something from these two people. Knowing that my alternative was to walk away made it even more fun. Recognizing that I had to be willing to walk away was fundamental to the negotiation.

The approach I took with the developer was to talk about everything except the home under consideration. In doing so, we found that we had some common ground and some common interests. The developer talked about his successes and was pleased to demonstrate his pride in the reputation he had established in the local area during the past fifteen years.

After almost two hours of pleasantries, I indicated to him that we were having this discussion specifically because of his fine reputation in the community with buyers with whom I already had talked. I also told him we were interested in buying his product, versus other available products, because of his reputation for honesty and quality. Unfortunately, I was not sure we could afford the unit we wanted. I advised him that my immediate concern was to figure out how I was going to let my wife down gently if he and I could not agree as I knew she would be disappointed. I told him that I was not looking forward to a potentially quiet three hour drive home with her, but it probably was my worst case scenario.

The result was that I sat in the outer office for about ten minutes while the developer and the VP of Sales negotiated a lower price for me. I was called back into the developer's office and advised that the unit previously had been reserved for someone at a lower price, but that person had not executed the final contract. As a gesture of good will, the developer was willing to sell us the unit at the previous price. Those few hours probably were the most lucrative two hours of my life. Those two hours of discussion turned the negotiation into a large payoff for all involved parties.

In contrast to the above satisfactory feeling, some twenty-five years ago I believe I made the biggest negotiating mistake of my life. I gave away something at the negotiating table without getting something in return. I agreed to pay an extra year of licensing fees. As it was at a reduced rate, it did not appear to amount to much in the context of the total agreement. I found out about one year later, what appeared to be a minor point during the negotiations could have been a deal breaker for the other party. Had the other party not gotten the additional licensing fees, irrespective of what they may have had to give in return, their bank would have withdrawn the offer to finance that party's leveraged buyout of another division of the company. In essence, there would not have been any possibility of the other party consummating their other deal. I still cannot believe and they "won" an enormous point without having to concede anything in return.

If our team had any inkling about the importance of this point to the other party, we could have gotten two or three concessions we wanted in return. Another lesson learned the hard way! You need to do your homework and obtain as much information as possible before the negotiations begin.

Something else to keep in mind is to remove personalities from the negotiating process. You may not necessarily want the people from the other team to become your "new best friends," but more than likely you will want to, or may have to, continue to do maintain a relationship with them. As a result, you will have to keep your personal feelings about the other people outside of the negotiations. Similarly, you will need to work on keeping your emotions in check, and out of the negotiating process. Usually, displays of frustration and outbursts of anger have no place at the negotiating table. These displays of emotion could cost you heavily in your ongoing dealings with the other party, and in an extreme situation, could cost you the relationship and the deal. These emotional displays also could be viewed as lack of control or lack of judgment translating into a viewpoint that you may be someone who may not be reliable in the long term.

Occasionally, a specific item is a deal-breaker for you, and if the other party demands it, you have to be willing to walk away. A highly charged tactic could be your only avenue at this point in the negotiations, but if it fails, you could be done without reaching agreement.

To illustrate this point, after four months of protracted negotiations to form a joint venture outside of the U.S. between two major corporations, one party continued to request something they had been advised was against the other company's corporate policies. The request was to allow the joint venture to use the other company's brand name on products the joint venture was going to produce for the aftermarket. Knowing that the requesting party already had told high level government officials they had a "deal," and therefore effectively had already committed to the deal, I took a calculated risk. I advised the requesting party again that their request was a "deal-breaker" and I could not understand why they would continue to request something they already knew would not be acceptable to the other party. Without another word I slammed my book closed, grabbed my briefcase, went to the airport and flew back to the U.S., leaving a corporate lawyer, as well as the other party, sitting at the negotiating table in shock. The next morning, my phone rang at home and I was requested to return to Mexico to "ink the deal." After an all night internal negotiation, the other party had concluded that their request was unreasonable. As stated earlier, there is always an exception to the rule, and you better be comfortable that when you take this approach, you may be walking away permanently.

In the long run, you will be far better off bringing the other party to their senses. You do not want to hammer the other party into submission. Even though this approach might be in line with other cultures' perception of the typical North American "deal maker," it does not serve any long term objective and certainly will not provide a foundation for a lasting relationship.

We need to explore this in a little more depth. In many cultures, North American negotiators are viewed as cowboys. The image is that of John Wayne riding in on his white horse, guns blazing away to eliminate the bad guys. In these cases, the approach is to save the day in less than five minutes by dictating the terms, or effectively, establishing the outcome without negotiating. Typically, the result from this approach is a short lived relationship at best. History has shown that relationships based on "win-lose" transactions will fail rather quickly. The "losing" party will direct their efforts and their energy on getting even to the detriment of everyone.

Early in my career, I negotiated a manufacturing licensing agreement which was very favorable to the licensee in terms of the benefits versus the costs. About two years into a seven-year agreement, the licensor had the opportunity to "level the playing field." The licensor had developed the next generation material used in the process. The new material offered significant cost savings opportunities in the manufacturing process. The licensee had no choice except to buy all of their raw material requirements from the licensor. You guessed it, the licensee ended up paying a premium for the new material which more than made up for what the licensor believed to be a shortfall in licensing revenue.

Another mistake I made at the negotiating table reinforces the point about walking away, and it supports the point that willing parties will find a way to come to a mutually satisfactory agreement. The incident resulted from my expressing a position in terms that were interpreted by the other party as "take it or leave it." In other words, their interpretation was that there were no alternatives "on the table." The other, more experienced party suggested that we adjourn for dinner and continue the negotiations the following morning. After dinner, the head legal counsel for the other party called me aside and, in a constructive manner, advised me that I had backed them into a corner and had upset several members of their team. As we both wanted to find a way to agree, his advice was that I begin the next morning's session with a restatement of our company's position. This approach would serve as a means of clarification and it would avoid unnecessary and potentially protracted negotiations over what should have been a non contentious point. Worst case, if not clarified, it could have resulted in termination of the negotiations.

A stalemate can result from a simple misunderstanding. Sometimes it can result from the fact that one party is so focused on their position that they are not communicating with the other. They may be listening, but they do not hear what is being said. There is a big difference between listening and hearing. If you are married, ask your wife to explain it to you some time, but be prepared for a long list of examples when you did not hear what she was telling you.

To break a "stalemate" and relieve the tension at the table, I like to use a joke to ease the tension. In those cases where it appears that there has been a breakdown in communications, I have used the following story with very successfully. Remember the whole idea is to get people to come to their own conclusion that they may be listening, but they are not hearing what is being said.

The story is as follows. An elderly woman goes into a store specializing in ice cream and tells the young man behind the counter that she is having a dinner party that evening for which she is preparing a very special dessert. As a result, she wishes to buy one gallon of chocolate ice cream.

The young man politely explains to her that of the thirty-one flavors that they advertise, he only has thirty flavors available. He clearly states that "there is no chocolate ice cream today." He then suggests that perhaps she could substitute one of the other thirty flavors for the chocolate. After reviewing the flavors on the board for a few moments, the woman says to the young man, "I'll just have one half gallon of chocolate ice cream instead of the gallon I originally requested." Being somewhat flustered, the young man calmly, but firmly states that unfortunately he has "no chocolate ice cream today!" Again, the elderly woman ponders the flavor board and very calmly says to the young man, "I tell you what, I'll just have one quart of chocolate ice cream." At this point the young man realizes that they are not communicating and decides to try a completely different approach.

"I have three questions that I would like to ask you," he says. "First, do you see the butternut ice cream on the flavor board?" When she replies "yes," he then asks her what flavor she would have if she took the butter out of butternut. "Nut," she says. "Good," he replies. "You've gotten the first one correct!" The second question is, "What would you have if you took the 'coco' out of coconut?" "Young man, that's simple," she answers. "Again you'd have nut!"

"Lady you are doing great, you've answered the first two questions correctly," the young man says. "Now here is the third question. What would you have if you took the 'f' out of chocolate?" The woman very indignantly answers, "Young man, there is no 'f' in chocolate!" The young man smiles. "Now you understand. That is exactly what I've been trying to tell you. Today there is no 'f' in chocolate."

At the same time, you have to be careful in assessing the situation to determine when humor is appropriate. Another mistake I made was to interject a humorous remark to break the tension at a meeting where I felt as though I was on trial before a board of high level executives at General Motors (GM) who were trying to determine whether I could be trusted to treat both parties in a fair, unprejudiced manner. I knew that given the opportunity I could be fair, so the situation seemed somewhat humorous to me. Apparently I did not assess the true level of concern to those seated around the conference table. The comment I made almost cost me the consulting job.

I had been hired by a major North American automotive supplier, for whom I previously had provided consulting services. They needed assistance in negotiations with General Motors to form a joint venture. My client had explained to the GM team members that they wanted to use a consultant, who had years of experience doing similar alliances for Ford Motor Company before retiring from Ford. I did not know it at the time, but there were some serious misgivings among the GM executives whether a Ford retiree could be trusted with information relative to future model plans and internal pricing for the automotive products under consideration. As a result, GM requested that I present myself to the team (with my client in attendance) to explain my background, my experience and my business approach.

I found myself standing at the head of a large conference room facing twenty-eight people – three from my client's company and twenty-five from GM. After everyone had introduced themselves, I realized that there were seven lawyers from GM present. My assumption was that GM was concerned about how I would be able to negotiate a fair agreement as I was being compensated by my client. I found out later their real concern was my former loyalty to Ford and the likelihood that I might disclose inside information to my Ford contacts. In any event, I totally misread the situation, and after briefly going through my background and my business philosophy, I ventured a small joke.

"If you feel that I cannot be fair to you at GM as I am being compensated by the other party, I have a suggestion that would level the playing field," I said, with a big smile. "You can both pay me!"

At that moment, I found out how a standup comedian must feel when a joke bombs and the room is deadly silent. You probably could have heard my heart beating, but I thanked everyone for their time and quietly took my seat. A few days later, my client called to advise me that we were going to continue as planned, but that they had spent the better part of two days explaining to their GM counterparts that I was only kidding and I really did not expect to be paid by both parties to ensure fairness. Talk about misreading a situation. Another lesson learned, and as I always say, "If you learn from your mistake it has been a good experience."

In contrast, no matter how attractive an offer may be, do not allow yourself to agree too quickly or the other party could feel dissatisfied. They might feel as though they have left something on the table. To reinforce this point, following is a role play that I have used in the past. The scenario is that an individual has a very clean, low mileage, imported sports car for sale. The vehicle is sitting in his driveway with a for sale sign indicating a price of $15,000. The challenge to one group is to negotiate the best price possible within fifteen minutes. The objective, of course, is for the seller to obtain the highest possible price, and for the buyer to obtain the car for the lowest possible price. At the end of fifteen minutes, each team indicates their final price and briefly describes the process how they got to that particular price.

The instructions to the second group of people is for the seller to only sell at the posted price of $15,000. The buyers in this group are told to buy the vehicle at the posted price of $15,000. There is to be no negotiation. When asked about their feelings regarding the process, all members of this group tend to feel as though they had left something on the table. The sellers felt like they had not set the price high enough, and the buyers felt like they overpaid.

In many people's minds, probably in most people's minds, negotiating is a confrontational process where at the end of the day, someone has to win and someone has to lose. This attitude can be seen from the inception of most negotiations where the parties position themselves on opposite sides of a rectangular table and set up another "chicken dance."

Imagine a pie in the center of the table with the objective of dividing it between the parties. If the parties are sitting opposite one another staring at the pie, each will be thinking of ways to cut the pie in such a way to ensure that their half is bigger than the other party's half.

To achieve true success that thinking has to change. In other words, the objective has to change from getting a "bigger half" of an existing pie, to an objective to work together to make the pie bigger so that both parties end up with a bigger piece of the pie than they could have on their own. The aim should be to change from a confrontational approach to one where the parties think creatively and where they collaborate, ultimately to the benefit of both parties.

To increase the chance of success, the physical setup has to change. In those cases where I am able to arrange the setting, I ensure that there is a round table where the parties have an opportunity to act as equals. There is no head of the table and no arbitrary "line in the sand." In those cases where a rectangular table is the only available option, ask the other party to make room for you on their side of the table so you can work together toward a better outcome for both of you. Explain that your hope is to combine your talents and resources and "make the pie bigger." At first this approach may not be credible to some people because of their perspective of negotiations as strictly transaction type events. So your first negotiation may be to convince the other party that you are sincere, that you are honest and that you really are trustworthy. In other words, you will need to convince them that this approach is not some new kind of negotiating tactic or trick to win something from them at the outset.

You've heard the expression "Silence is golden." While at the negotiating table, silence has more value than you can imagine. For many people, staying silent is one of the most difficult aspects of negotiation. I've never understood why some people feel as though they have to fill every void in a conversation. As you think about this point, you will soon realize you can learn a lot about the other party, about their wants, and their needs just by listening instead of talking. Similarly, you have to realize the other party probably is doing exactly the same thing when listening to you and your team members.

Information is power at the negotiating table. Don't forget the earlier example where I gave something away with nothing in return as I had no clue how important it was to the other party. The point is that the more information you have, the better the outcome for everyone. Also remember to ask open ended questions, questions that do not allow for a simple "yes" or "no" answer. Finally, remember to let the other party do the talking.

You also need to learn to recognize body language signals. They are like "tells" at the card table. You should pay attention to what the other party may be telling you through body signals. For example, someone leaning back away from the table probably is telling you that they do not buy into what you are telling them. Nervousness often is displayed through constant swinging of the legs. Also, you may want to pay particular attention to the other person's eyes. For the most part we can control the muscles in our lower face, but eye movements are more difficult to conceal. That is why many professional poker players wear dark glasses at the table. Pay attention to what kind of messages you may be sending to the other party through your own body language.

Everything in Life Is Negotiable

As I wrote earlier in this chapter, most North Americans are uncomfortable negotiating. This character trait appears to be recognized in most other areas of the world. As a result we are viewed as fairly easy to negotiate with as we want it to be over quickly. To do so, the tendency for many of us is to "split the difference" and make the issue go away. In many parts of the world, knowing that about North Americans enables the other party to use the clock very effectively against us. I remember many years ago, each time I would go to Japan, the other party would graciously offer to provide transportation to and from the airport and to confirm my hotel and airline reservations. In many cases these offers were sincere as they wanted to provide assistance as a means of building the relationship. In other cases, however, it was a clever way to gain information about my scheduled departure so the negotiations could be put off until late in the visit in the hope that the clock would serve to force me into "splitting the difference."

I finally learned to avoid this pitfall and to eliminate the clock from the negotiations. I would book an open-ended return trip, and would advise the other party that I did so to allow enough time to complete the negotiations while ensuring sufficient time for a more favorable outcome. It was amazing how the timetable changed on the ensuing visits. Negotiations took place from the time I arrived until the time I left instead of being condensed into the last morning.

Another lesson I learned through a variety of mistakes, is that when dealing with other cultures you should not overestimate English comprehension based on English speaking skills. I am not demeaning other cultures as their understanding of English typically far exceeds our ability to speak their language, but there are subtleties and innuendos in English that go beyond the dictionary's definitions of words. In the same way, we are disadvantaged by not being able to speak or comprehend the other party's language. This gives the other party the opportunity to sit in the same room with you and strategize about a response to a particular point while listening in to your discussions among your team members.

In those cases where we may understand a few words, we often do not comprehend the true meaning of the words. We need to learn and to understand the cultural subtleties and linguistic nuances that other cultures use. For example, when dealing with the Japanese, the words "Hai, hai" often will be used to signify "We understand." Due to our lack of understanding of the exact meaning and use of those words, we could take it to mean "Okay" or "We agree," only to find out later that there was no agreement, just an understanding of the particular point made during the negotiations.

Roger E. Axwell's book, *Do's and Taboos of Humor Around the World,* contains a treasure of stories reinforcing the point that verbal misunderstandings often lead to difficult, but often humorous situations. To reinforce this point, here are a few examples from his book.

"Words are the common denominator in our communications. Spend a few years in international travel or international business, and the impact and the worth of even a single word becomes startlingly clear."

"For example, during World War II, a misunderstanding over just one word—the verb 'to table'—created great debate and ill will. According to the memoirs of Sir Winston Churchill, he and his staff were discussing with their American allies whether they should "table" a certain issue. However, when Americans "table" an issue, it means they set it aside for consideration at a later time; when the British "table" an issue it means to place it on the table for *immediate* discussion. "A long and acrimonious argument ensued," Churchill wrote, until finally the two sides discovered their respective cultures had contrasting definitions for the same term."

"People who travel overseas take comfort when visiting other English-speaking countries such as Great Britain, Ireland, Australia, and so on because there is no language barrier. As we learned earlier from Mr. Churchill's story about the verb "to table," however, that is not exactly the case. There are hundreds, even thousands, of significant differences between British English and American English. In fact, there are large dictionaries now available listing the different word usages between the two. One prominent example occurs when we visit England and rent an automobile. First, as most people know, the British drive on the left side of the road.

But that's not the only difference between our two countries. As it happens, *every part* of an automobile seems to have a different name from those we use in the United States. For starters, you don't "rent" a car in England; you *hire* a car. Then, in Britain the hood is called the *bonnet*, the windshield is called the *wind-screen*, the dashboard is the *fascia*, the muffler is the *silencer*, the trunk is the *boot*, and on and on."

"Here are some other stories about confusing words from Tom Newman:

- In Venezuela, he saw a billboard advertising the classic movie *Grease*. The huge sign announced John Travolta was starring in *Vaselina*.
- In Italy, his friend was struggling to remember and say the word for 'onion.' He stammered for a while and finally said: 'It is the fruit that makes you cry.'
- Walking along the Yangtze River in Shanghai, China, a young Chinese man approached him and asked in English: "Do you want me to cut your face?" Happily, he soon discovered that the Chinese man was asking if he wanted him to cut out a silhouette of his facial profile!"

To at least partially offset your language disadvantage, I would urge you to hire a competent translator, and to ensure that the translator is briefed on your deal as well as your expectations from him or her in the negotiations. I also would urge you not to rely on the other party's translator. Further, you need to ensure you are comfortable that your translator not only speaks both languages fluently, but also is well versed in the subtleties and nuances of the languages. To accomplish this objective, the translator needs to be briefed and rehearsed before joining the group at the negotiating table.

Finally, you need to be very explicit about your expectations and very specific about the translator's role in the negotiations. For example, you should make it clear that you expect the translator only to translate. Explain that their responsibilities do not include negotiating on behalf of either party. Their sole job is to make certain your positions are conveyed accurately to the other party, and the other party's positions are made clear to you.

I recall an incident where language and interpretation was not the real problem. The translator our team employed was very proficient in Italian and in English. The problem resulted from the fact that for several days we were unaware that the translator was using his own discretion to determine what was important, and therefore, what was being translated. He also was putting his own spin on the meaning and intent of certain statements as he did not comprehend the intricacies of the business. Unfortunately for both parties, this situation did not become known for several days and resulted in lengthy discussion of points where there truly was no disagreement. The manner in which it became obvious to the parties that the translator had evolved into the role of mediator was not humorous. Effectively, it resulted in many hours of unnecessary negotiations and came close to negatively having an impact on a good relationship.

I had made a lengthy, five minute explanation of a somewhat complex and difficult point. It may have been the most difficult point in the entire agreement. The Italians appeared very intent as the translator explained our position. At that point, the Italian team discussed what they had heard in a very expressive and overtly emotional manner among themselves for the next twenty minutes. They then explained their position to our translator for approximately five minutes.

The translator turned to us with a serious look on his face, and very succinctly said that our counterparts were "having some difficulty accepting your position." After the shock wore off, we excused ourselves from the room to evaluate the situation. Upon returning, we excused the translator, managed to explain our point directly to the Italians and eventually reached agreement. All this was accomplished in roughly ten minutes. At the conclusion of that session, the translator was eliminated.

Another situation occurred during a dinner one evening in the mid 1990s. I was heading a team representing a North American joint venture company considering a three party venture in China.

As the head of the team, I was considered the guest of honor and always was served first, most of the time by the local mayor or other high level dignitary. That probably does not sound like a difficult situation, but you have to understand that by custom no one else at the table is allowed to eat until the "guest of honor" has tasted and complimented the food. The other party's translator presented a wonderful description of the meal of which we were to partake.

Apparently, the fish being served could only be caught at night in water about four hundred feet deep. Once caught, the fish had to be kept alive in frigid water until it was to be cooked. As a result of the difficulty in catching the fish, and then ensuring that it was kept alive, it was rare to have the opportunity to taste this delicacy. Later I was told that each fish cost more than US $400.

After the fish was presented to the table, and after the appropriate speeches were made, the mayor of the town placed the head and the tail of the fish on a plate and presented it to me. He made the presentation with a toast to our future relationship, which in a positive sense stated that our business relationship should have a good beginning and a good ending. As the head and the tail of the fish were the beginning and the ending of this rare fish, it was only appropriate they be given to the "guest of honor." Everyone else at the table, of course, was served a beautiful portion of fine looking white fish — boneless at that. I was very much looking forward to tasting this rare and exotic fish. While looking down at the head and the tail and trying to come up with the appropriate and gracious words of thanks, I noticed the mayor looking longingly at the portions on my plate. As I firmly believe everything in life is negotiable I thought this might be an opportune time to negotiate for what I really wanted — a different and more appealing piece of fish.

With that thought in mind, I asked the translator to tell the mayor I was honored to be given these delicacies and I agreed with his analogy to the business we were considering. I then went on to say that since we were considering a joint venture, it would be more appropriate for the mayor to share in the head and the tail, while I shared in his portion of the fish. In that way we both would be starting off working together from the same base. From his facial expression, and the fact that he absolutely cleaned his plate, I felt comfortable that the negotiations were off on solid footing. After two days of discussions, we departed on very pleasant terms and with a warm invitation to return at any time. Ultimately, a different location was chosen for a number of business reasons. Nevertheless, we had established a good contact for possible future opportunities in China.

Remember that negotiating can be fun, so do not be intimidated by it. Most people enjoy the game. Most cultures outside of the U.S. consider negotiation as an integral part of any transaction. In some countries they will not even sell to you if you do not negotiate. It is a way of life and something that comes naturally in many cultures. It can be considered bad Karma, or bad luck to sell to you without first negotiating. In extreme circumstances it is a cultural abomination, and even an insult, to some people if you offer to buy something at the stated price.

In preparing for a negotiation, you should focus on the fundamentals:

Understand the Basics

- Everything in life is negotiable
- You don't necessarily get what you deserve; you will get what you negotiate
- Providing satisfaction leads to a "win-win"
- Willing parties will find a way to come to a mutually satisfactory agreement

Do Your Homework

- Understand your most desired or acceptable result
- Identify the essentials (i.e. the "must haves")
- Develop alternatives and build in flexibility
- Gather information

Information – A Key Ingredient in Successful Negotiations

- Information is power—the more you have, the more your cards are worth
- Develop information about the other party's stated needs
- Understand your own team members' needs and priorities
- Gather information about the other negotiators; understand their personal needs
- Understand the other party's corporate culture
- Develop sources throughout the other party's organization; develop a network of contacts

Some of the best lessons in life come from the mistakes we make. If you make a mistake, and you repeat it, then shame on you. Remember, "First time, shame on me, second time shame on you, and there ain't no third time." If, however, you learn from your mistake, then it is not really a mistake. The mistake becomes a lesson in learning and you are better off from the experience.

Let me give you a simple example. I learned early on in life to find out as much about the other party as possible before trying to negotiate with them. Gathering information is just one step in doing your homework in preparing for negotiations. Remember not to overlook finding out as much as you can about whoever will be participating from your side of the deal. One of the many mistakes, I've made over the years, relates to not understanding the needs of some of the players on my own team.

One of the initial steps in the process of trying to establish a joint venture in Mexico to manufacture automotive parts was to evaluate potential alliance partners. A team composed of top management personnel (including the general manager, director of manufacturing, human resources director, controller, director of product development, etc.) from one of Ford's manufacturing divisions arrived in Mexico on a corporate jet. At that time, I was the lowest-ranking member of the group and already had been in Mexico for about a week setting up meetings with the top four Mexican conglomerates. In addition, I found myself in the unfortunate role of handling hotel accommodations, dinner reservations and all other logistical details to keep the Ford management personnel stroked and smiling.

To my dismay, when the group was checking into the hotel, the clerk advised the general manager that there was no reservation for him. The worst part was that the desk clerk also stated that the hotel was full and maybe they could find him a reservation elsewhere in Mexico City. I suddenly saw my career flash before my eyes. The general manager, red-faced, glared at me with the veins standing out in his neck and wagged a finger in my face. "How the hell did that happen?" he growled.

I quickly explained that I had checked to ensure that the number of rooms was correct, but admittedly had not checked by name. I then suggested that I get everyone something to drink at the lobby bar while I straightened out what I believed to be an oversight. As it turned out, it was nothing but a typographical error in the general manager's last name. Someone had typed the letter "G' instead of "T," a keystroke that almost caused me to have a real stroke! Once corrected, everyone seemed to settle down, and I thought the issue was behind us. Everyone but the general manager, that is. Every time he got frustrated with any part of the negotiations, he brought up the incident as an example of whether I had gotten into the details in sufficient depth. Each time, I got what I fondly refer to as "management lecture number 3." Simply put, "management lecture number 3" is, you better pay attention to all details, including whose feathers might get ruffled easiest.

The lesson from that experience is to understand which shelf of the coop people are sitting on and that you had better stroke all the people above you. Let's face it, the lower your level in the coop, the more people potentially get to dump all over you! As I was on the lowest shelf of this particular coop, I stood to get buried. As it turned out, once the deal was signed, I was cleaned up and was promoted to the next management level.

Role Play

- It will help you eliminate surprises
- It will help you further develop your skills
- It will help you achieve better outcomes

- It will help you better understand yourself, and how you are perceived by the other party
- It will help you develop a comfort level

Role playing is like a rehearsing for a show. The person who is to lead the negotiation should sit with a few people and outline your company's position on any given negotiating point. The other people in the room should offer counterproposals that might be anticipated from the other party. As these practice negotiations advance, positions and responses need to be evaluated constructively by the group so the negotiator gains a comfort level with the positions and alternatives. I always used to get people who had been involved in other alliances, as well as a lawyer or two, to participate in the role playing exercises.

Before you do a role playing exercise, do your homework. Essentially you will have to outline the key topics for negotiation. For each topic, you should then outline your negotiating position as well as what you believe to be the other party's position. At this juncture, you should set up a meeting with representatives from all the affected disciplines within your organization. Next, you and your entire team should meet together with the affected parties in your organization to enable you to get a good read on their reactions and responses to the various negotiating topics and positions. This approach will help you to establish a unified stance from your side of the negotiations and preclude "second guessing" at the conclusion of the negotiations.

By reviewing each item in this manner, you should be able to uncover any sensitive areas that may not have been obvious to you, as well as uncovering potential "deal breakers" for the other people on your side of the "deal." Finally, the group may provide you with some new negotiating strategies and/or alternatives to further assist you in reaching a satisfactory agreement.

There always are situations that do not follow the rules. Negotiating is an art rather than a science and one that you refine over time. As each negotiation is unique to the deal as well as to the people at the negotiating table, the key to success is to remain flexible. Above all you must be creative in your approach to resolving what may appear to be insurmountable obstacles.

In 2002, I was called in by a major automotive company to help sell a supplier company owned by two brothers. I refer to them as the Marx brothers as they managed to keep me laughing during our working relationship. The Marx brothers' company was in Chapter 11, and their principal customer, one of the big three domestic auto manufactures who I will refer to as "Big Mama", wanted to transfer all the Marx brothers' business to their competitors while assuring uninterrupted supply to themselves. As a result of their long-term relationship, "Big Mama" also was hoping that the Marx brothers could realize some money out of the sale of their company. This was anything but a normal situation. As in all negotiations, there are unique circumstances surrounding "the deal." In retrospect, the unique aspects of this situation made it very frustrating and required that we develop a somewhat different approach if we were to succeed and get paid our fees.

As it turned out, the negotiations were not only interesting, but also turned out to be more fun than expected. The Marx brothers had been urged by "Big Mama" to hire my organization as opposed to other capable companies to help them consummate a sale. As a result, it wasn't difficult to convince the Marx brothers that we were best suited to serve their needs. The point that persuaded them to hire us was that "Big Mama" wanted us to do the job, and therefore, we had a leg up on making it happen. "Big Mama" represented more than 90 percent of their business at that point, and therefore, carried a big stick.

Second, compensation for "the deal" had to be approved by the bankruptcy judge considering all the claims of the creditors. As far as I can remember, the judge proclaimed our fees as being "totally out of the realm of reality." The fact that our fees included a "success bonus" tied to the actual sales price almost got him climbing over the bench. Ultimately, the judge agreed to the fee structure, but it was anything but a level playing field during that negotiation.

Talk about "positioning." I had a stiff neck from looking up at the judge while being lectured about taking advantage of the

Marx brothers. My best guess is that he was upset that our fees for one deal probably approximated his annual compensation.

The next step was to determine exactly what the Marx brothers' company had to sell. Now here came the fun part. The Marx brothers' had sold and leased back all the company's assets. That's right, not only did they sell their buildings, machinery and equipment, but they even sold and were leasing back the office furniture.

At this point, you have to wonder what they have for sale. Obviously there's no good will, so you look for unique technology, patents or anything that might provide a competitive edge to a potential buyer. Well, guess what — there was nothing to sell. It didn't take long for our "analysis of the obvious" to become clear. All that remained was the order book from "Big Mama," and "Big Mama" was becoming more nervous with each passing day. Keep in mind that "Big Mama" could transfer the business (i.e. the order book) anytime they wanted. While we were negotiating with the Marx brothers and the judge, and gathering facts about the company, roughly one-third of the order book had been given to the Marx brothers' competition. Not only was the deterioration in business making the creditors more nervous, but the "success fee" portion of our compensation also was deteriorating rapidly.

It was not a very good situation for anyone. To make it work would require some creative thinking and perhaps some new dance steps. As a first step, we decided to approach "Big Mama" and try to negotiate a temporary hold on transferring any more business from the Marx brothers. Being a very large corporation, "Big Mama" had several layers of purchasing personnel involved in the dance. "Big Mama" also had several policies and procedures that would come into play. "Big Mama" told us what we were asking for was "totally unrealistic." This comment was very similar to the judge's reaction to our fee structure. We knew we had been put in the middle of the dance floor among the "warring" parties. We had nothing to sell but the "order book." The Marx Brothers' competitors were talking to "Big Mama's" purchasing people to try to get the remainder of the "order book." The judge thought we were taking advantage of the Marx Brothers. Time was running out on the bankruptcy filing. It appeared that we were going to end up in line with the creditors at a giant "chicken dance" in front of the judge if we didn't come up with a new approach.

We finally realized that the path to success was to remove ourselves from the role of "negotiator" and position ourselves as "mediators." To accomplish that objective, we first went to "Big Mama," who initially requested that we handle the deal. We convinced the head of purchasing to put a temporary freeze on transferring any more of the Marx Brothers' "order book" without his prior approval. That approach was non-threatening as it left him in control while benefiting us by taking control away from the individuals at the lower levels. The rationale we used was that if the transfer of business continued unabated, concerns could be raised about "Big Mama's" loyalty and relationships with long-term suppliers in troubled times. Also the Marx Brothers would not be kept whole if their business completely eroded while they were looking for a buyer.

As a second step, we went to the bankruptcy court. We advised the judge that we were negotiating with several potential buyers, but we needed four more weeks from the creditors. Without the four weeks, the creditors would end up with nothing. Given the four weeks, the creditors potentially could receive twenty to thirty percent of their claims contingent upon the final sale price. As a third step, we advised the potential buyers that we had to agree by a certain date or the "order book" would be broken up among several of their competitors. We wanted everyone to focus on what they had to gain from a sale of the Marx Brothers' company, and that we were their best chance for bringing it all together.

Ultimately, it worked to the benefit of all parties. We stepped back and let "Big Mama's" head of purchasing become the chief negotiator with the buyer for the "order book." He even provided some price relief. The judge became the chief negotiator with the creditors to extend the time line. To us this was a thing of beauty. We were called into the courtroom full of creditor representatives and told by the judge to finish the deal in four weeks or all bets were off. The potential buyers of the Marx Brothers' company concluded negotiations with us in record time.

From the time we changed our role from being in the middle of the dance floor to sitting on the sidelines and guiding the dance, the deal was concluded in less than four weeks. The best part was that along with preserving our compensation package, which the judge signed off on, the Marx Brothers were able to retain some money. To the Marx Brothers, this result was like the Phoenix rising from the ashes. The key to success in this negotiation was to remain open-minded, flexible and creative in trying to find acceptable solutions for everyone involved. The real breakthrough came by enabling other people to take control of the negotiations while we orchestrated the dance. The whole point of this story is to recognize that if the parties are willing, and if they are made aware of the benefits to them, agreement can be reached.

Finally, there are circumstances that are just plain "no win." To illustrate the point, I will describe a situation that arises periodically, which doesn't follow any rules and for which I am still at a loss to negotiate successfully. It is a negotiation that I refer to as "damned if you do; damned if you don't!" I've known my wife for over 40 years, and every time she tells me that she's going to a new hair stylist or that she's going to try a new hairstyle, I feel like running away from home. It is the one situation that I have determined has no correct answer and is non negotiable. Here is what happens. My wife goes out and gets a new hairstyle. She cannot wait to return home and ask the dreaded question, "Honey, how do you like my new hairdo?"

Think about it for a minute. There is no correct answer to that question. You may or may not take the time to look up from the sports channel on TV and say something like, "Wow, I really like that" or "You look wonderful." The response you get probably will be something like, "What was wrong with my old hairstyle?" Maybe you'll even get speech number 23, which goes something like, "Well, if my old hairstyle was so bad, why didn't you say something before?"

On the other hand, if you take a minute to focus on the new hairstyle before committing yourself to a well thought out compliment, it's likely to be interpreted as a loss for words. That translates into, "You really hate it, don't you?"

As I said earlier, the question "Honey, how do you like my new hairdo" is a "no win" negotiation for men. Fortunately for me, it has become somewhat of a joke in our home. When my wife goes out to get her hair done, I usually run in the closet and hide when she arrives home.

To help reinforce some of the things you already have learned about negotiating, here are a few examples of what you can accomplish. It has been done before. There are no fixed rules. You can be creative. It can be fun. It can save you money.

The next several pages contain several real life stories demonstrating just how much fun negotiating can be when you understand the fundamentals. These stories also reinforce how much better the outcome can be when you avoid approaching negotiations from the perspective that someone has to win at the expense of the other party. Instead, approach it from the standpoint of "making the pie bigger" so that everyone ends up with a bigger piece of pie at the end of the day. Remember you are striving for a better outcome and a better, longer lasting relationship.

EVERYBODY WINS

This story reinforces two fundamentals of a successful negotiation. First, you can save money if you ask questions. Second you can build a better, longer lasting relationship with the other party while doing so. The idea is not to hammer the other party into submission, but to ensure that both parties walk away satisfied because there was something in it for everyone.

Here is what took place. I had my semiannual air conditioning system checkup by the company providing me this service since the day I bought my home. This was the same company that did the initial installation. After the technician departed, I noticed the system was taking a long time to cool down, a problem that did not exist before the service call. Another service contractor came by within an hour – great service – and indicated we needed a new thermostat. He returned the next day, performed the necessary work and departed without leaving a bill.

A few days later I received two bills for the same work, both of which I thought were too high. I called the company and we discussed the fact that there were two bills for the same work. When they indicated they were going to send a revised bill I asked that they review the charges as I believed they were too high. I also mentioned that as they had done the initial installation, and had been servicing the system since day one. I was disappointed that the thermostat had to be replaced so soon. I also pointed out that since we have had a great multiyear relationship I would appreciate it if they would review the charges before sending the new bill.

The next morning they proposed to reduce the charges by approximately 35% which was more than I anticipated. Taking that as a good starting point, I asked if they could do a little better. The discount grew by another 10% which resulted in an even larger discount than I hoped for. At that point I told them I valued our relationship, I looked forward to continuing to do business with them and thanked them for their consideration.

The outcome was that I asked and saved some money. They negotiated, and they have a satisfied customer who will recommend them to other potential customers. The point is, both parties felt they had won something and both felt satisfied.

✡ ✡ ✡

A TOUCH OF CREATIVITY MIXED WITH A BIT OF HUMOR

Recently, I accompanied my wife on a shopping excursion to acquire some "post Christmas super savings." It wasn't exactly what I wanted to do that day, but figured it might provide an opportunity to have some fun and do some creative negotiating somewhere along the way.

In one store, we went up to a table with a large sign announcing "Selected Items 60% Off." As the table contained some candles that my wife wanted, she thought that she would be saving a significant amount of money by buying ahead for next year. My spin was, "This is how we go broke saving money." Just to keep the peace, I kept that thought to myself.

When the clerk began to ring up the candles, the discount was only 25%. With a smile on my face, I asked the clerk to accompany me back to the table. I then asked that she read me the sign as I must have misread it or had a "senior moment" as I thought the items on the table were "60% off." She pointed out that only "Selected Items" were "60% off."

Again, with a smile, I said, "That's what I read too," and since I "selected" these items, don't you think I should get "60% off?" I was just having some fun, as I already was bored with the shopping. When she stopped laughing, we returned to the register at which point she took another 25% off the candles.

Not a bad return for a bit of humor. What is more important, however, it again supports my negotiating tip, "You only get what you ask for," or "If you don't ask, you don't get."

✭ ✭ ✭

ANOTHER SHOPPING ADVENTURE

A friend of mine, with whom I have shared many negotiating tips and stories over the years, recently related an interesting experience with me.

Since my friend spends much of her time negotiating with real estate developers and builders, we often share stories about her most recent experiences in the world of negotiations. Apparently she has shared my negotiating tips and stories with her children, the youngest of whom was thirteen years old when this negotiation took place.

Here is what happened. Mom and daughter went shopping for some shorts which were on sale at a local department store. The sale was advertised as "Big markdowns – 33 1/3% off." Eventually the daughter found the exact shorts she wanted which were marked down from $30 to $20. Just like the ad said, a 33 1/3% discount.

Before going to the checkout counter with her shorts, the daughter spied a sales rack with a sign proclaiming "50% Off." Not wanting to pass up the opportunity to get more for her money, she meandered off to check out the shorts. Much to her amazement, there was an identical pair of shorts hanging there with a $20 price tag, but on a sales rack declaring "50% Off."

Guess what! The daughter, who has now become one of my new negotiating heroes, marched up to the register and indicated to the salesperson that she was ready to buy the shorts for – you guessed it – $10. Now here is how it played out. The salesperson told the young woman that if there were more of the same $20 shorts on the "50% Off" rack, she would honor the $10 price per pair. They walked over to the rack where they found several more pair, two of which happened to be the young woman's size, but in different colors.

Not wanting to pass up the opportunity to leverage her negotiation, she took all three pair for a grand total of $30, or the equivalent of one pair at the original price. It proves again that "you only get what you ask for." Try it! You have everything to gain and nothing to lose.

CREATING OPPORTUNITIES AND SAVING MONEY

Recently, all of us have felt some pressure from the economic environment in one way or another. The problem is that in many cases we do not recognize the opportunities resulting from the situation, nor do we take advantage of these opportunities.

Let's face it, none of us are immune to the impact of a soft economy. What we often fail to recognize is that the companies providing our goods and services also are feeling the effects. Once you accept that as a fact, you begin to realize that the circumstances should make these companies more flexible and more willing to negotiate. They know, and you need to understand, that retaining a good customer is far more cost effective than trying to gain a new customer.

In this regard, and in the spirit of customer focus, some companies are providing rewards to customers on an unsolicited basis. I can personally vouch for companies like Nordstrom and US Bank credit card services. Having said that, most companies are not particularly proactive in handing out financial incentives just to retain customers. To access opportunities for saving money, it is the customer that must be proactive – and that means you. You have to believe in two fundamental guidelines that I preach *ad naseum*: (1) everything in life is negotiable and (2) if you do not ask for something, you will not necessarily get it.

I recently posted an article on www.beyondthechickendance.com recommending that you contact all those companies providing your cell phone, internet and cable services to request a reduced rate. I had a few responses from people in the US and the UK telling me stories of their success and how good it felt. Their stories motivated me to test the water with my own service providers again.

In doing so, I discovered some new information. My first contact with each company was with the Customer Service Department. In each case what they offered did not meet my "wants." After a couple of calls, it became apparent to me that the customer service personnel were not delegated sufficient authority to meet my "wants." After thinking about it, I called each company back and asked to be connected to their "Customer Retention Department."

In all three cases the conversation was brief, the personnel were very helpful and the results met or exceeded my "wants." Net, net, with just three phone calls to the right people, in a matter of less than thirty minutes I saved about three hundred dollars a year. That may not seem like much money, but it amounts to a rate of over six hundred dollars per hour. I don't know about you, but I would sign up for a job that paid me that much in a hot minute!

TRY IT; IT WORKS

It does not matter whether I am with my pal Hooch, a West Highland Terrier, on the beach, out shopping with my wife, in a local restaurant, in a foreign country, or just casually chatting with someone, I always am watching people and how they approach the opportunity to negotiate. The one thing that never ceases to amaze me is how many opportunities to achieve better outcomes are overlooked just because someone has not made the effort to negotiate a better "deal." Observing others negotiate, or pass up the opportunity to do so, is part of my personal continuing education program.

As everyone who has ever spoken with me knows, before the conversation goes on very long, the subject of negotiation will come up. Once that door is open, you can be certain you will hear about my firm beliefs that: "Everything in life is negotiable" and "If you don't ask, you won't get."

Well, here is the good news! During the past few weeks I have received several calls from friends, former business associates and professionals with whom I have made contact on line. The recurring theme from these people has been a resounding and enthusiastic, "It works, I tried it and it works!"

One gentleman from the UK indicated he was successful in negotiating with two of his utility providers and with a maintenance company. The net result was a savings of between two and three hundred pounds ($300 - $475) per year on an ongoing basis.

Another party indicated that they had achieved a fifty per cent rate reduction from their VOIP provider for the next year. He was so enthusiastic about the outcome, he was about to repeat the process with his internet and cable providers. I have since learned that he managed to negotiate discounts from all of his service providers.

These people have adopted a new approach based on the premise that "everything in life is negotiable and if you do not ask, you do not get." Each of them has been very excited about the results, and could not wait to tell me their success story. Along with saving money and feeling good, they indicated they were going to apply their new approach to all of their business dealings as well as in their personal life.

I don't know who was more excited, them or me. The fact is that successful negotiations lead to far more than saving money. If you haven't tried it, what are you waiting for? Your worst case scenario is you may spend a little time and effort on something to improve your skills so you can do better next time. "Go for it!" Again, you have everything to gain and nothing to lose!

WHY YOU NEED ALL THE INFORMATION

In ancient Greece (469 - 399 BC), Socrates was widely lauded for his wisdom.

One day an acquaintance ran up to him excitedly and said, "Socrates, do you know what I just heard about Diogenes?"

"Wait a moment," Socrates replied, "Before you tell me I'd like you to pass a little test. It's called the Triple Filter Test."

"Triple filter?" asked the acquaintance.

"That's right," Socrates continued, "Before you talk to me about Diogenes let's take a moment to filter what you're going to say. The first filter is Truth. Have you made absolutely sure that what you are about to tell me is true?"

"No," the man said, "Actually, I just heard about it."

"All right," said Socrates, "So, you don't really know if it's true or not.

Now let's try the second filter, the filter of Goodness. Is what you are about to tell me about Diogenes something good?"

"No, on the contrary..."

"So," Socrates continued, "You want to tell me something about Diogenes that may be bad, even though you're not certain it's true?"

The man shrugged, a little embarrassed. Socrates continued, "You may still pass the test though, because there is a third filter, the filter of Usefulness. Is what you want to tell me about Diogenes going to be useful to me?"

"No, not really."

"Well," concluded Socrates, "If what you want to tell me is neither True nor Good nor even Useful, why tell it to me or anyone at all?"

The man was bewildered and ashamed. This is an example of why Socrates was a great philosopher and held in such high esteem.

It also explains why Socrates never found out that Diogenes was sleeping with his wife.

INFORMATION IS POWER

A man is getting into the shower just as his wife is finishing up her shower. About that time, the doorbell rings.

The wife quickly wraps herself in a towel and runs downstairs.

When she opens the door, there stands Bob, the next-door neighbor.

Before she says a word, Bob says, "I'll give you $800 to drop that towel."

After thinking for a moment, the woman drops her towel and stands naked in front of Bob.

After a few seconds, Bob hands her $800 and leaves.

The woman wraps back up in the towel and goes back upstairs.

When she gets to the bathroom, her husband asks, 'Who was that?"

"It was Bob the next door neighbor," she replies.

"Great," the husband says, "did he say anything about the $800 he owes me?"

Moral of the story:
If you share critical information with others, you may be able to prevent avoidable exposure.

THE MORE INFORMATION, THE BETTER THE OUTCOME

A priest offered a Nun a lift.

She got in and crossed her legs, forcing her gown to reveal a leg.

The priest nearly had an accident. After controlling the car, he stealthily slid his hand up her leg.

The nun said, "Father, do you remember Psalm 129?"

The priest removed his hand But, changing gears, he let his hand slide up her leg again.

The nun again said, "Father, remember Psalm 129?"

The priest apologized saying, "Sorry sister but the flesh is weak."

Arriving at the convent, the nun sighed heavily and went on her way.

On his arrival at the church, the priest rushed to look up Psalm 129.

It said, "Go forth and seek, further up, you will find glory."

Moral of the story:

If you are not well informed, you might miss a great opportunity.

✯ ✯ ✯

THE CLOCK STRIKES AGAIN

Another situation I found myself in many times resulted from my frequent trips to Japan during the 1970s and 1980s to negotiate a series of license agreements. To make it easier on me, the Japanese company often would greet me at the airport and deliver me to my hotel so that I could relax before dinner. During the two hour trip from the airport, my host typically would offer to assist in reconfirming my return flight. During 1970s and 1980s, most overseas flights required reconfirmation by phone at least 48 hours before departure.

In preparation for the discussions, I would plan three or four days in Japan to allow for two or three long days at the negotiating table where a significant number of items could be resolved. Usually, I found myself meeting with the host company for the entire time, but in the beginning what I did not realize was that the real negotiations did not take place until the last meeting before my scheduled departure. That is when only a few hours remained before I headed off to the airport.

It was not until this situation occurred several times, that I finally figured out "the clock" had become a major player at the negotiating table. Once the "light came on" and I recognized the tactic, I always booked an "open return" and so advised the host company when I arrived. My new tactic was to remain in Japan "until we agree." Not surprisingly, by eliminating "the clock," negotiations began after dinner the first evening and continued throughout each day until I departed.

Over time, I learned two key lessons: (1) do not let arbitrary deadlines affect your negotiations and (2) do not to let the fact that you are on the other party's turf work against you.

✧ ✧ ✧

THE KEY TO BETTER AND LONGER LASTING RELATIONSHIPS

This should help you remember everything you have read thus far about negotiating and about building better relationships.

By now you should recognize that every day we are surrounded by opportunities to negotiate. Whether you realize it or not, you are negotiating all day every day at work, at home and elsewhere. Take a minute and reflect upon a typical day in your life. You probably have negotiated with a customer, a supplier, your boss, another department or another employee. Then you go home and negotiate with your spouse, your children and your pet. Let's face it, you have even been negotiating through traffic on your way home! It never ends!

So, here are some questions to ask yourself. How well did you do at your last negotiation? Was your desired outcome successful? Did you feel good after the "deal was done?" How can you become a more successful negotiator? What tips can be learned to achieve more satisfactory and longer lasting results so that you do not have to confront the same hurdles repeatedly?

To begin with you need to understand some of the fundamentals. The starting point is your own approach to negotiations. If you view negotiations as "win-lose" transactions, they may feel good to you in the short term if you are the "winner," but over time reality will set in that the outcome was unbalanced, and not necessarily fair to the other party. You soon will come to the realization that the other party was not satisfied, and as a result, they will continue to negotiate with you to gain back what they think they have lost.

The key to a successful negotiation is to ensure that each party recognizes they have had to make concessions and that they have gained some concessions from the other party. In other words, at the end of the day, both parties should feel as though they may have given up some things, but they also have gained some concessions in return. Only then will you have the foundation for a long lasting successful relationship that benefits everyone.

WIN-WIN IS A LIFESTYLE FOR SUCCESS

I have been following Lonnie Sciambi's blog for a couple of years as he always offers good advice in a succinct and easy to understand manner. His latest post on "win-win" gets to the core of *Getting from You and Me to WE* so I had to include it verbatim. You can get more good advice from Lonnie at www.thesmallbusinessfor

"As with most of my blog posts, a recent encounter with a client and one of their key suppliers triggered this one. The supplier had negotiated a "sweetheart deal," hammering out an almost-untenable agreement with my client, who needed the critical service that the supplier provided.

Further, at every turn, the supplier was determined to drive the relationship and ensure that they "won" every point from proving that it was the fault of the client's drawings that caused the supplier's quality problem (a real stretch) to marking up and getting every last dollar from the client, a fledgling company operating on relatively thin financing. The upshot? With additional financing, we found a better solution by moving the service in house and rendered the supplier relationship an afterthought. Key to this supplier (also an entrepreneur himself) was that he "grew up" in a huge corporation.

It is often said that we are the product of our environment; that what we are often the sum total of our experience. Nowhere is that more true than with entrepreneurs.

Many entrepreneurs, like our supplier example, grew up in a big company culture, learning real-world business skills, often, from, politically charged situations, driven by folks with personal and professional agendas. In most of these environments, the object is to win (whether or not that particular "win" benefits the company) and the opponent (often in a corporate turf war) loses. In effect, a "zero sum game," which is the way our supplier operated. In this environment, the idea of "win, win" is, virtually, unheard of. Yet, the key to entrepreneurial success, and maybe even life success, is "win, win" in all relationships. And, it is here that the fledgling entrepreneur, often, has to unlearn bad habits and learn new ones.

For some folks, "win, win" is some Pollyanna-ish notion that can't exist in the "dog-eat-dog" business world. And, they could not be more wrong. Having negotiated hundreds of deals from the complex – acquisitions, capital investment, joint ventures, outsourcing - to the straightforward – contractor, distributor, employment relationships, the common point of all success is that both parties have to walk away feeling that they had "won." Maybe not all they could, but enough so that the other guy could feel the same way.

But for many entrepreneurs, this type of thinking is foreign from the way they were "brought up" in the big company mindset. So, for you folks, and as a refresher for you others who already believe in and practice "win, win," here are some key ways to ensure all your negotiations and relationships end up that way.

✵ ✵ ✵

KNOW WHAT YOUR OBJECTIVES ARE

Going in, know what's absolutely essential, what's important and what's just "nice to have." Then you know what points you have to hold firm on, what points can be negotiated and what ones don't really matter.

✯ ✯ ✯

PUT YOURSELF IN THE OTHER PERSON'S POSITION

This is where "win, win" begins. Try to understand what their objectives are, what they need to get out of the negotiation or relationship. Try to put their objectives in the same three categories as yours above. Hopefully, you can both achieve what is essential.

✯ ✯ ✯

GIVE A LITTLE, TAKE A LITTLE

Negotiations and relationships are built on this concept. There are always "tradeoffs." Let the other party feel like they have "won" some of their points. If they walk away from the table with a deal, where they felt like all they did was "give," it will come back and haunt you later, trust me.

✯ ✯ ✯

KEEP THE RELATIONSHIP OPEN, HONEST AND RESPECTFUL

Incredibly important. To keep relationships going requires that when screw-ups occur, as they will always, that there is honest accountability and "give and take," to ensure that steps are taken to not have them repeated. No blame game, just honest admission and the spirit of "moving forward."

"Win, win" is not a one-time thing. It is a business lifestyle. Learn it and live it and your success will follow."

✯ ✯ ✯

THE DEAL MAKER

I recently heard a story from someone I had spoken with about asking for something in return before you give something away. I explained to her that negotiating is like trading, it is not a giveaway process. This is a great story.

This woman, who clearly was uncomfortable negotiating, took her SUV in for an oil change and was told it was time for some regularly scheduled maintenance. The dealership – one of two owned by the group – quoted a price more than $400 for the scheduled maintenance plus the oil change. My friend paid $29.95 for the oil change and said she would think about the other recommended maintenance as she did not happen to have $400 available for what she considered to be discretionary spending.

About two weeks later, a card arrived in the mail from the other dealership in the group offering the identical scheduled maintenance at a somewhat lower price. My friend took that as an opportunity to negotiate, and continued to talk to the second dealership. She explained that she was very upset as the first dealership had tried to take advantage of her by charging full price for the scheduled maintenance and full price for the oil change. This approach was a great opening tactic. Then the negotiations began in earnest.

The net result was that the scheduled maintenance was performed at about a $100 savings (more than original discount offered by the second dealership) and the price was further discounted by virtue of my friend getting additional credit for the $29.95 payment she already had made for the oil change.

For someone who was reluctant to negotiate, getting a discount of over $125 versus the original quote is a major success. All I can say is that Jan has earned a place on my list of "New Negotiating Heroes."

✣ ✣ ✣

KNOW WHEN TO FOLD AND WHEN TO RUN

My father-in-law, Charlie, came to the US when he was just thirteen. After going through processing at Ellis Island, he ended up in McKeesport, Pennsylvania to join the Hungarian community there.

Charlie already had the entrepreneurial spirit at that young age, so he started off by delivering water to the workers at the steel mill. According to the family stories, like most entrepreneurs, Charlie's business ventures often failed, but he dusted himself off and always pursued another dream. As the stories go, some of his more memorable ventures included owning and operating the "Flora Dora" hotel, restaurant & bar in Pennsylvania, owning a butcher shop in Dearborn, Michigan and ultimately becoming a Quality Control Inspector at Ford Motor Company.

Charlie was not only an entrepreneur at heart, but he also was a very adaptable and creative individual. For example, when he applied for the job at Ford, he asked what they needed. A great example of customer focus. The response was "quality control inspectors." Without a clue about what that entailed, Charlie convinced them he was an expert in quality control inspection and retired from that position 17 years later.

The best story, however, relates to his "pre-Flora Dora" days. Not one to overlook an opportunity, Charlie began to brew his own beer and market it to his customers at the "speakeasy" he was running in PA during the "Prohibition" era. After all, he was committed to focusing on his customers' needs, and it just happened to be during prohibition, so why not fill their need for beer. Apparently his beer was among the best being brewed during that time, and the word spread quickly. It spread all the way from PA to NY, which got Charlie an invitation to meet with Dutch Schultz, a recognized underworld personality who loomed large in illegal beer and liquor distribution among other enterprises.

Recognizing an opportunity for growth, Charlie went off to negotiate with Dutch in New York City. Unfortunately, it was another dream that did not work out for him. After a successful negotiation with Dutch in the morning, Charlie heard on the radio that Dutch had been gunned down just a couple of hours after their meeting. Charlie, immediately recognized a lost opportunity, and decided not to stay in town to try a negotiate a deal with the new "boss." The way the family tells it, he did not pause to review the alternatives. Instead, he hightailed it to the train station and left on the next train out before someone came looking for him.

Along with all his other attributes, Charlie was smart enough to recognize that in this situation the risks outweighed the potential rewards. His quick assessment was that it had become a "no win" situation for him and it was time to walk, or in this case, run away from the "deal." In his mind, Charlie had a clearly defined outcome and he had the confidence and clarity to walk away.

50 WAYS TO LEAVE THE NEGOTIATING TABLE

Remember the Paul Simon song, "50 ways to leave your lover?" Although the song did not outline 50 distinct ways to leave, it did present some catchy lines that soon became popular. In case you cannot remember them, here are a few that seem to be the most popular:

- "You just slip out the back, Jack."
- "You don't need to be coy, Roy."
- "Hop on the bus, Gus."
- "Just drop off the key, Lee"

Similarly, when you are in a situation during negotiations that you know is not reasonable, or if is not at all possible to agree to a specific point, you have to recognize that there are many – perhaps not 50 – ways to say no.

Here are a few ways to say "no" while leaving the door open for the other party to modify their position.

- I don't think I can sell that, but I'll ask.
- I'll try to find out, but that could put me in the middle.
- I don't think there's much of a chance of getting that approved, but I'll ask.
- I'll let you know, but I don't have high hopes.
- I don't have the authority to agree to that.

You have to be careful not to use this last response very often or you will be sending a message to the other party that they may be negotiating with the wrong person.

Saying "no" in a more subtle fashion, will accomplish several objectives:

- You will avoid raising expectations in the other party's mind that their request will get satisfied later.

- It prevents you from having to give up a significant point on the spot.
- It keeps the negotiations open.

THE ULTIMATE NEGOTIATION

Last October, actually on Halloween Day last year, I had the privilege of sitting in the US Supreme Court in Washington. This was not just a normal visit for me as my niece, Valerie, was arguing a case that morning and I had come to observe, and along with other members of our family, lend some moral support.

The building is very majestic and awe inspiring. It is more than that; it is overwhelming. As you approach the stairs leading up to the building, you cannot help but think about the fact that you are entering the most powerful court in the country.

On the front of the building it says, "Equal Justice Under The Law." Around the walls of the building are sculptures of the people who historically have played an important role in the justice system of our country. On either side of the main steps are very large, seated marble sculptures. On the left is a female figure, the Contemplation of Justice. On the right is a male figure, the Guardian or Authority of Law.

Just in case the thought did not register with you, the "chicken dance" begins before you even get into the building. You are about to enter the inner sanctum where it is the "court of last appeal." The game ends here. There is no higher power; there is nowhere else to go.

At the east end of the Great Hall, oak doors open into the Court Chamber. This dignified room measures 82 by 91 feet and has a 44-foot ceiling. The raised Bench behind which the Justices sit during sessions, and other furniture in the Courtroom are mahogany. The Bench is winged shape to optimize sight and sound advantages. The Bench is elevated, I would guess, about eight to ten feet above the area where the lawyers present their arguments. Another step in the "chicken dance" to demonstrate the justices power over the Court. As my niece is only about five feet tall, I can only imagine how it felt looking up at the justices during her entire argument. That is the supreme positioning step in the "chicken dance."

Sitting in the Supreme Court chambers as a member of the audience is overwhelming in and by itself. I was thinking about how overwhelming it must have been for my niece who was sitting up front waiting for the justices to appear from behind the curtain. Oh yes, that is the next step in the "chicken dance." The nine justices do not enter the courtroom individually, they appear all at once when the twenty foot (my best guess on the height) red curtain parts and the justices step forward en masse.

The justices, of course, are wearing their black robes, and again, look very intimidating standing in a row behind their seats. They reminded me of giant bats about to swoop down and suck the blood out of anyone daring to expose themselves. Being there on Halloween only added to the image I had in my mind at that point.

Once they are seated, the pace really picks up for the dance and the steps become more intricate. The attorneys arguing cases before the Court occupy the tables in front of the Bench. When it is their turn to argue, they address the Bench from the lectern in the center. A bronze railing divides the public section from that reserved for the lawyers.

Each of the attorneys has only thirty minutes to present their case. The process is unlike any other courtroom procedure you may have seen on TV or in real life. In the Supreme Court, the attorneys do not have the opportunity to present complete arguments as the justices are continuously firing questions at them, sometimes in mid-sentence. Not only that, but the justices interrupt one another by asking questions of the presenting attorney before that attorney has had the opportunity to finish their answer to the previous question. Sometimes, the justices even fire questions at one another or make comments to one another while the attorney is trying to speak.

To say the least, it was very impressive to observe the inner workings of the Supreme Court. It was even more impressive to watch my niece, Valerie, argue her case there. I believed she had done a masterful job in presenting her argument and that she had maintained her composure under a very heavy barrage of questions from up above.

Without going into all the case details, suffice it to say that if she won, it would set a new precedent for the US legal system. Valerie, as well as many of the other lawyers in her office and some family members, believed that the likelihood of winning her case was minimal at best. To add to the suspense, the Court had until June of 2012 to hand down the decision.

Time passed slowly for Valerie and for the rest of us until one day in March. Valerie was notified on March 21, 2012, that the Court had decided 5 to 4 in her favor. Not only had she won her argument, she did so against the Solicitor General of the state of Michigan who was supported in his argument by the Solicitor General of the United States. If that were not enough, she established a precedent further ensuring everyones' right to "effective legal counsel." It was the culmination of about 8 years of dedicated effort and hard work against almost insurmountable odds, but she added some new steps to her version of the "chicken dance" and succeeded.

Winning an argument in the Supreme Court, the highest, strongest, most powerful court in the United States has to represent the ultimate negotiation.

If you would like to learn more about this case, go to the link shown below which summarizes the case on the American University Washington College of Law "Criminal Law Brief Blog."

http://wclcriminallawbrief.blogspot.com/2012/03/lafler-v-cooper-scotus-extends.html

✯ ✯ ✯

ARE NEGOTIATIONS EVER OVER?

I used to think that once the formal negotiations were concluded, the contracts signed, and any mementos of the "deal" exchanged, that the "deal" was done. In reality, the formal negotiations may have been concluded and the agreements may have been committed to writing and signed, but in many cases the real negotiations have just begun. In some cases, this may result purely from a cultural norm, but more often than not it results from having to deal with real life situations.

The reality is that no agreement can anticipate every possible circumstance or situation the parties may face during the term of their agreement. Lawyers do their best to provide contingencies in the agreements in anticipation of change, often adding to the frustration of the business people. Nevertheless something usually will arise that previously was unforeseen at the negotiating table. The key to success is to ensure that the parties have a good enough working relationship to enable them to use their combined "expertise" to resolve the "unforeseen" issue. Doing so will not only help enhance the relationship, but typically will ensure that the parties derive benefit from the outcome over the long term.

The worst possible scenario is one where one or more parties run to review the exact verbiage in the signed agreements each time an issue arises. This approach is a clear indication that the agreements may have been signed, but that one or more parties were not entirely satisfied or comfortable with the outcome. It even may be an indication that one party feels as though "they left something on the table" and here is an opportunity to get something back to "level the playing field."

In each case, it is a clear indication that the negotiations have not been concluded to the satisfaction of all the involved parties, and left unchanged, the likelihood of a successful lasting relationship is compromised. It is highly likely that the relationship has been doomed from the moment the agreements were signed. The agreement more than likely is being viewed by one party as a mechanism to conclude the relationship and move on.

At the conclusion of formal negotiations, we always presented a nicely bound copy of the agreements to all involved parties to commemorate the "deal" and to provide a reference document for the record. It always was our hope that no one would ever have to refer to the document to resolve an issue or to confront an unexpected change in circumstances affecting the relationship or the business. Instead, we hoped that any unforeseen event could be dealt with outside of the agreements themselves and that the parties would "put their heads together" to the benefit of everyone involved.

If you have to refer to the contract to deal with change or an unforeseen event, your relationship already is in trouble, and the long term outlook for your relationship is not very promising. It would be much more effective to resolve the issue by working together to come up with a creative solution that satisfies everyone involved.

Everything in Life Is Negotiable

Now that you have finished reading this part of the book you should have become much more aware of how much of your life is invested in negotiating. You also probably are more aware that every facet of your daily life involves negotiating in one fashion or another. It is a "womb to tomb" process so you need to get comfortable with it.

I believe that the more you learn about negotiating, and the more comfortable you become with the "ins and outs" of negotiating, the more fun you will have. You also will achieve better outcomes and feel much better about the results. I am sure you by now you have a better understanding of the process.

Because negotiations are the foundation in building all relationships and alliances you need to remember the "Power Negotiating Tips" which are referred to throughout this chapter. If you remember to use these tips you will be pleasantly surprised by the results.

Just to help you reinforce them, I have provided a synopsis of these 16 powerful tips below**With rare exception, everything in life is negotiable.** You need to recognize that you are involved in negotiations throughout the day at work and at home. At work you negotiate with your boss, your peers, your customers, your suppliers, etc. At home you negotiate with your spouse and your children, and if you admit it, some of you even negotiate with your pets. At the same time you have to be alert to the fact that there are some "no win" situations" that you need to acknowledge before you get in too deeply.

If you do not ask for something, you will not necessarily get it. You need to recognize that you only will get what you negotiate; you will not necessarily get something just because you think you deserve it.

Don't ever give something away without asking for something in return. Realize that you will have to make some concessions to reach a satisfactory agreement, but always point out to the other party when you have made a concession, so they recognize value in your concession.

Information is power. Ask open ended questions to obtain as much information as possible. Do not ask questions that can be answered with a simple "yes" or "no." Do not just listen to what the other party is saying, make sure you hear what they are saying. Also do not forget to focus on body language as that is an integral part of the message.

Never accept the first offer. Do not agree to something too quickly or the other party could feel as though they left something on the table. This could cause them to dedicate their time and energy on getting something back later in the relationship, more than likely to the detriment of both parties.

To achieve a successful outcome, all parties to the negotiation have to feel as though they have won something. For all parties to win, you need to **"make the pie bigger"** so that when you cut the pie, everyone ends up with a bigger piece. The whole idea is to view negotiations as everyone gaining from the transaction as opposed to "someone has to win and someone has to lose."

Role playing is like rehearsing for a show. The more you rehearse the better the outcome. Role playing prepares you for negotiating in many ways. It will help you to: (1) eliminate surprises, (2) further develop your skills, (3) better understand yourself, (4) understand how you are perceived by others, (5) develop a comfort level and (6) achieve better outcomes.

The better prepared you are, the more fun you will have once you are at the negotiating table. Understand that all parties to the negotiation have specific wants and needs. Also understand that all parties are under pressure to achieve a satisfactory outcome — at least from their perspective. Further understand that all parties will have to make concessions to achieve a satisfactory outcome.

Recognize the body language of others at the negotiating table as well as that of other people in the room. The signals are like "tells" at the card table. Also think about the signals that you and your team members may be sending out to the other party. Remember that body language is part of the communication process, so do not just listen to the words being spoken.

To break a "stalemate" or **to relieve tension in the room, take a break from the negotiations and use humor.** If you can tell a story that is relevant to the point you are trying to negotiate so much the better. When using this approach, however, be careful that you do not misread the situation or tell a story that offends someone.

Remember that "**silence is golden.**" Sometimes silence has more value at the negotiating table than anywhere else. Do not feel as though you have to fill every void in the conversation as you may be giving away information that is better left unsaid. Remember that information is power so the more one party has, the stronger their position.

Avoid falling into the pitfall of "splitting the difference" just to make the issue go away or just because you are uncomfortable with the negotiations. Never be the first one to offer to "split the difference." Let the other party be first with that offer as it indicates a willingness to do so, and could establish a pattern that could become useful to you in your positioning.

When dealing with other cultures, do not overestimate English language comprehension based on English speaking skills. There are subtleties and nuances in the English language that go far beyond the words themselves. Similarly, be careful that you truly understand the meaning of specific words and gestures of other cultures before agreeing to something. The use of a trained translator, working specifically for your team, is critical in many foreign environments.

Time tends to be a critical factor in every negotiation. **Do not set arbitrary deadlines** as they will result in less than optimum outcomes. To the extent possible, eliminate the clock from the negotiations.

Negotiating is an art, not a science. **There are no set rules or magic formulas in the negotiating process.** While there may be many similarities between one "deal" and the next, each "deal" is unique. To ensure the best possible outcome, recognize that both parties are under pressure. It is not just you! So, stay alert, stay creative and take your time.

The reality is that **no agreement can anticipate every possible circumstance or situation the parties may come across** during the term of their agreement. Inevitably, something will come up that was unforeseen at the negotiating table. The key to success is to ensure that the parties have a solid working relationship to allow them to combine their expertise to resolve the "unforeseen" issue. If the relationship is to succeed over the long term, the whole focus should be for the parties to put their heads together to make "the pie bigger" so that everyone ends up with a bigger piece of pie at the end of the day.

✯ ✯ ✯

CHAPTER 5

EVERYBODY WINS

I have been fortunate to have participated in the development of several successful alliances. In addition, I have been fortunate in developing many long lasting relationships and friendships that continue to this day.

I discovered early on, however, that the excitement and enthusiasm leading up to the formation of an alliance often turns into frustration once the contracts are signed. One hurdle that seems to frustrate the parties is the seemingly disproportionate amount of resources and time required to ensure success. I also discovered that failure often is caused by the parties anticipating too much in the way of benefits to be gained from the "synergies" that were expected by combining the strengths of both parties. Let's face it, these comments originated in the context of business alliances, but they apply equally as well to personal relationships. Dedicated effort and commitment by both parties are required if the relationship is going to succeed.

While I used to think that the successful alliances were due to my strategic thinking and creative negotiations, to be realistic about it, success was in large part due to timing and overall economic conditions. Above all, however, the commitment of the people that worked in these successful alliances was absolutely critical to success

I'd like to share a story about the various stages of an alliance that I think will tie together most of what you have read in this book. While it illustrates what went right and what went wrong, I hope you will see that alliances can and do work when the involved parties are flexible enough to adjust to change and when they are committed to succeed. Finally, I hope you'll remember this story so that you can take what others have learned to help you in your own relationships.

In the late 1980s when joint ventures and acquisitions were gaining popularity in the automotive industry, Ford Motor Company and Magna International, Inc. formed a joint venture to manufacture and paint front and rear bumpers and fascias. Back then, Magna was a successful automotive supplier with operations in the United States, Canada and Europe. Sales were slightly more than $750 million a year. Initially, the joint venture's production was dedicated primarily to support Ford requirements.

When I first had the opportunity to participate in the "chicken dance" with the people from Magna, I found them to be young, enthusiastic, confident and very entrepreneurial. In contrast, most members of the Ford team had been around the automotive industry for many years and were steeped in policies, procedures and processes, only some of which were well founded.

The dance went on for about a month while we at Ford performed many analyses whether the benefits of an alliance with Magna outweighed the risks of giving away "our secrets." Over the next 14 years we learned, and hopefully you will see, that it was fortunate for both parties that the scale tipped in favor of forming the alliance. Not only did it contribute to the "learnings" for each party, but it also turned out to be financially profitable for a number of years.

It all began with one manufacturing operation in the US to produce parts for Ford as well as other car companies in North

America. Both Ford and Magna contributed equity and knowledge to the venture consistent with their respective ownership positions and strengths. In addition, Ford contributed some technology to the venture which Ford believed was proprietary.

One of the interesting things I observed is how the management positions played out during the negotiations. Logically, they ended up reflecting the parties' own perceived strengths and corporate personalities. Magna wanted control of manufacturing; Ford wanted control of the financials. As it turned out, Magna staffed the key positions, and Ford initially took a "hands off," oversight approach in hopes of learning from the entrepreneurs. Once we signed the deal, the fun really began.

Magna, the entrepreneurial company, operated decentralized operations. It owned a majority interest and had control of the operations. Ford was focused on financial reporting and centralized controls. Given these radically different corporate cultures, the early stages of the alliance were awash with "learnings" on a day-to-day basis. While the venture was evolving, some of the lessons were painful for both parties. For example, Magna was charging down the road to procure the latest and greatest equipment from Germany while Ford was still analyzing machinery and equipment alternatives. By the time Ford reached a conclusion, orders had been placed by Magna and the machinery already was under construction. Ford executives would have preferred a different source for the machinery, but changing suppliers would have resulted in significant additional costs, which was unacceptable to both parties.

There was a series of heated meetings between the parties to try to find a way to better serve both parties' needs on future capital investment decisions. Magna could not wait for Ford's analyses to be completed, reviewed, updated and re-reviewed. Ford was not accustomed to sitting on the sidelines and learning about things after the fact. By the time the manufacturing operation was built, many accords had been reached. I thought we all were on the same page and on our way to success, but not many people at Ford shared my comfort level. I also was accused of thinking too much like those "entrepreneurs" at Magna, which frankly, I considered a compliment.

In a few years, the manufacturing operations were running smoothly, the joint venture was about to show a profit, and the parties were reasonably content with one another. During this time, Magna continued to grow by expanding its operational base and by diversifying into non-automotive businesses such as restaurants and real estate development, which were totally unrelated to their core business. As a result, they became somewhat "cash strapped" and were looking for creative ways to support continued growth.

One of the operations in Canada that Magna was in the process of constructing was Polycon, a factory that would be capable of producing products similar to those being produced in the Ford-Magna joint venture company. With a flourish, I proposed to Ford that they not only participate in Polycon, but that they use this situation as an opportunity to accomplish two more things. First, since Magna was looking for capital, why not increase the Ford equity position in the existing joint venture to gain a larger share of the profits? Second, why not look for other opportunities within Magna's broad-based operations as we already had a going relationship with them? Eventually, Ford took a minority interest in Polycon as well as one of Magna's tool-building operations, Tycos Tool, which already was making tools for the initial joint venture company as well as some wholly owned Ford operations. This move provided Ford with the ability to reduce its tooling costs and tool build time, thereby gaining a competitive advantage.

As a result of complexities associated with running these three geographically separate operations, Ford and Magna concluded that a small management team should be established to oversee the three venture companies. The team was to be staffed by the two parties with Magna filling the manufacturing related functions and the CEO's position, and Ford filling the financial functions and the President's position. The intent was to let the new organization run the joint venture companies without undue interference from the Ford and Magna.

The "chicken dance" now began all over. It was even more fun for me. Picture this scenario. You are the one who has encouraged both parties to broaden the scope of the original venture by expanding it to three operations. Even though the parties had found a way to work together with one joint venture operation, this new entity created a whole new set of problems and "learnings." Now, every time a problem arose, my phone would ring and I would find myself in the role of mediator. Even though it was a "chicken dance" of sorts, at the beginning it was more like a "cock fight." Until people figured out their respective roles and realized they needed to work as a team, it appeared that the new layer of management was not such a good idea after all. The new entity, Conix Corporation, probably should have been named "Confusion Corporation," because confusion seemed to be its defining culture during its initial phase.

One of the key things that people transferred from the parent companies had to learn was that their allegiance belonged with their new employer, the joint venture company. The parent companies are important, but they become like shareholders — needing to be satisfied, but not be involved in day-to-day operations. Again, with time there were a few personnel changes in the top positions at Conix. Also, due to promotions, transfers and other corporate decisions, some of the people at the parent companies, who previously were involved in overseeing Conix's operations, moved to other positions within their respective companies. These changes provided Conix less daily oversight by the parent companies which enabled them to exercise more control over their own operations.

After a year or so of smoothing out the bumps in the road, Conix was making progress. Although it had not yet developed its own robust culture based on the best aspects of each of the alliance partners, it seemed to be headed in the right direction. Unfortunately, as a group, the two bumper and fascia companies, and the tooling company were not yet profitable, and the alliance partners were getting restless.

It was about that time in 1991 that I retired from Ford with the idea that I was going fishing. As it turned out, that retirement — the first of three before I got it right — lasted all of two weeks. At the end of the second week I had established a consulting firm. I'm sure you won't be surprised that my first client was Magna, which needed some help dealing with the people at Ford. Later, both Ford and

Conix became clients. For the better part of the next two years, as a consultant to Magna, I worked as an interface with Ford on items related to Conix. My other major responsibilities included taking the lead on negotiations to resolve contractual and issues related to performance on a multimillion dollar paint system.

In early 1993, as a result of personnel changes at Ford and Magna, the opportunity arose to fill some of the key management positions in Conix. Again, timing, market circumstances and some plain old good luck intervened. After several months of negotiation between the alliance partners over their expectations of, and compensation for, the new leader of Conix, a deal was struck with a friend of mine, John Tobiczyk, to become the new president of Conix.

As I was involved in brokering the deal, I could not have been more delighted that John was taking over leadership of Conix. He brought knowledge, experience and common sense to the table. He had previously worked at Ford and understood how Ford processed data and made decisions. He also had worked in several smaller, more entrepreneurial companies and understood how they operated effectively. Even better, he had manufacturing and engineering expertise in the specific processes employed at Conix. John also was a strategic thinker, and was committed to the philosophy that the employees should participate in the decisions affecting their company, as well as participating in the profits of their company.

I am convinced that without John's leadership, Conix would not have achieved the success that it did over the next eight years. The personal and professional attributes that he brought to the company were critical to Conix's growth and success. These attributes are critical to the success of any company, irrespective of its size, as they distinguish the difference between leaders and managers. In addition, John's compensation was tied directly to Conix profits, and as a result, he was not beholden to Ford or Magna.

By 1995, under John's leadership, Conix had developed its own culture. As it evolved, the Conix culture embodied the best of both alliance partners as well as John's beliefs from over twenty years experience in various operating environments. It fostered an entrepreneurial spirit, delegated authority to the people running the operations, involved people in the planning and decision-making processes, emphasized training and shared profits at all levels of the organization. It also embodied the principles of trust and accountability. While some structure was added, lean manufacturing methods were being practiced throughout the organization, not just in the manufacturing activities. These methods included elimination of waste and reduced response time to internal and external customers. By then Conix had become profitable and was being viewed by the alliance partners in an entirely different light.

Meetings between Ford and Magna were more positive, the parties were learning from one another and some aspects of Conix's operations were being viewed as the standard for Ford and Magna's wholly owned operations making similar parts. Transparency to both of the alliance partners was in place; there were no hidden agendas. Pre-meetings with members of the board were the key to Conix's ability to run its own business within the approved business plan levels. What a difference from the early stages of the alliance! In my mind the name of the joint venture company went from "Confusion Corporation" to "Summit Corporation," as it was meeting or beating its objectives. Conix's sales base was being diversified to include GM, Chrysler and some of the Japanese car companies producing vehicles in North America. Product lines also were being expanded.

In addition, Conix was exceeding profit targets by a wide margin. To the best of my recollection, in John's second year as President of Conix, the team delivered profits roughly fifteen times the target, an amazing accomplishment.

What were the lessons learned during the initial years of the alliance?

- Patience and commitment of resources are required over the long term.
- Communication among the affected parties at all levels of the organization is necessary.
- Differences in corporate cultures can present significant obstacles to success. Partners should adopt the best elements of each party's culture.

- The new organization should be left to run its operations without undue interference from the alliance partners.
- Compensation should be related to the success of the alliance company, and not to the alliance partners' practices.

Conix truly had evolved into a different entity. I was beginning to think that my consulting services might not be needed much longer and again was thinking about retiring. What I didn't recognize was that my next retirement was almost five years away.

In 1995, to meet the automotive manufacturers' requirement for suppliers to establish a global presence, John and I went to Europe and found new customers with a need for Conix's products and services. The alliance partners were enthusiastic about the idea and willing to support the expansion. It's amazing what eight years of working together, trusting each other and accepting the other party's point of view will do to enhance a relationship. Of course, the fact that the alliance was profitable and able to fund the expansion out of its own cash flow certainly helped.

By late 1997, Conix had two operations up and running in Europe. The alliance now was composed of five operations, one in the US, two in Canada and two in Europe. The lessons learned during the formative years of the alliance had been broadcast throughout the operations, Conix had its own culture different from those of its alliance partners, successes at one location were shared with the others, the business planning process was being used in every operation, and for the most part the alliance was funding its operations from its own cash flow. At this point, the alliance partners had taken a "hands off" approach and were overseeing Conix strictly through its Board of Directors.

Conix was doing all the right things and the alliance partners had learned to guide it rather than trying to run it. Although some of the lessons came at a price, and the relationship between the alliance partners often was strained in the early years, patience, commitment and trust resulted in success. From its inception in 1987, in a period of twelve years, Conix's annual sales grew tenfold.

While Conix was expanding in Europe, Ford decided that some of its parts businesses should be spun off into a separate entity. In the period 1996-97, Ford formed Visteon. In the early 1990s, GM and Chrysler already had spun off their own parts operations. GM formed Delphi and Chrysler formed Accustar. The strategic purposes of these "spinoffs" were to lower costs and become more competitive with independent part supplier companies to supply other automotive manufacturers as well as themselves. Longer term, the objective was to sell some or all of these operations to generate cash to support their core business of designing and manufacturing vehicles.

This signaled a change in "vision" at Ford. Ford had moved from the "growth through acquisition and joint venture" mentality that permeated the automotive industry for about a decade to one of refocusing on the core business. As part of its change in vision, about fourteen years after the initial "chicken dance" with Magna, the alliance was about to be undone. Sometime in the middle of 2000, Ford sold its interest in Conix to Magna and took with it a series of "learnings," as well as a significant amount of money. Magna also took away a significant number of "learnings," acquired several profitable "going" operations, and gained a significant amount of business it otherwise might not have gotten. It was a "win-win" outcome.

At this point you might be asking yourself if the alliance really had been worth it given the growing pains, the hiccups and the resource commitments required for Conix to achieve success. My answer would be an emphatic and resounding "YES!" Even with the startup problems, which gave many people heartburn during the alliance's formative years, the "learnings" that could be used in other operations had ongoing value. In addition, there were significant benefits to both Ford and Magna that were derived from the alliance including a better understanding of the inner workings of each other's company and a closer relationship between the companies.

Magna gained access to:

- Business within Ford that might not have been attainable
- Ford technology
- Ford systems, processes and methodologies
- Another source of capital funding when required
- Management resources
- Better understanding of one of their major customer's project and business review process
- Sharing of risk

Ford gained access to:

- Business to supply other vehicle manufacturers that might not have been achievable
- Lower wage rate operations
- Lower cost structure operations
- The inner workings of a more nimble, entrepreneurial company's methodology
- Management resources
- Sharing of capital expenditures to fund expansion of the parts business
- Sharing of risk

There also were benefits to the communities where the manufacturing operations were located. Each of these operations employed several hundred people, some of whom may not have been employed had the alliance not been formed.

EPILOGUE

Today the global automotive industry faces a new set of challenges and opportunities. Demand for cars, SUV's and light trucks dropped significantly from peak industry volumes due to several significant factors including:

- Higher prices at the gas pump
- Deteriorating consumer confidence
- Higher unemployment levels
- Consumer reluctance to make high end purchases
- Intensified competition due to increased foreign entries
- The two-edged sword of improved vehicle quality and reliability leading to longer vehicle life cycles
- Deteriorating global economy

These factors have recently exacerbated the decline of the US-owned automotive companies. For the past twenty-five years or so, increased competition, pricing pressures, higher fuel economy and improved quality levels from some foreign automotive manufacturers have hurt the US companies' standings in the global marketplace. Ford's U.S. market share has declined from about 25 percent to around 15 percent. Since 1982, GM's market share had fallen from about one half of the US market to roughly 25 percent.

To put this drop into perspective, based on unit sales, Ford used to be the number two automotive manufacturer in the world, second only to GM. By 2007, Ford ranked fourth, behind GM, Toyota and Volkswagen.

In 2008, GM slipped into the number two position behind Toyota. Finally, the domestic U.S. market used to be the largest in the world. Today, that position has been taken over by China. By structuring to "spin off" some of its parts businesses and starting to refocus on its core business of manufacturing vehicles, Ford began laying the groundwork to solidify its business base. Eventually, by selling off some of its parts manufacturing operations, Ford gained cash to use for other purposes, such as funding the development of new vehicles and new technologies required for Ford to be more competitive.

Without the Government bailout of GM and Fiat's takeover of Chrysler along with a Government infusion of cash, the US auto industry might have had a completely different landscape today.

Remember that during the 1980s and 1990s acquisitions were in vogue in the automotive industry. During that period, some of the "experts" were predicting that ultimately there would be fewer than ten major automotive producers in the world. Some went further and predicted that there might be as few as three to five survivors after the acquisitions and consolidations were done. Also remember that Ford was an integral part of the acquisition frenzy, having acquired Aston Martin, Jaguar, Land Rover and Volvo.

Ford's decision to concentrate on its core business and divest of some of its parts operations eventually led to its thinking about its vehicle business in a different light. Ford realized that the capital required to create new products and remain competitive in all its vehicle operations outweighed the benefits and synergies to be derived from some of its acquisitions. I'd also like to think that some of the lessons learned in their many alliances were helping to influence their thinking.

Ford successfully sold Aston Martin, Jaguar and Land Rover. Later it sold Volvo. It appears that these actions have generated cash to help Ford bring out a stream of new vehicles with enhanced product content, and with product quality equal to or better than its Japanese competitors. Of even more consequence, it appears that the capital generated, in conjunction with negotiated lines of credit, allowed Ford to become the only U.S. owned automotive company not requiring "bailout" money from the taxpayers. That's good for Ford, its shareholders and for us, the taxpayers.

In conclusion, I would say that Ford has learned well and is applying those "learnings" as it moves forward to address the new challenges it faces in the changing economy, the global marketplace and in the face of increasing government regulation. The lessons Ford learned should help sustain it and help it to succeed.

On July 22, 2009, in an article entitled "Ford on Pace for Turnaround," Forbes reporter Joann Muller stated that "Ford Motor Company has done a good job keeping it's eyes on the road during a difficult stretch, as it's domestic rivals veered off into bankruptcy." How was Ford able to stay on track while it's domestic competitors had to use our taxpayer dollars to stay in business?

My response is fairly simple. Ford has a vision, they have an effective business plan to support the vision and they are implementing strategies to achieve that vision. It really gets back to the fundamentals that provide the foundation of any good business as taught in "Business 101." It wouldn't surprise me to see a case study evolve rather quickly as a teaching aid to those still interested in perpetuating the free enterprise system.

My conclusions about Ford are based on basic business principles. I am convinced that Ford has refocused on their core competencies.

To support this conclusion, consider the following reported data:

1. Ford continues to improve their customer satisfaction ratings, with Ford's ratings now exceeding those of Honda and equal to or slightly higher than Toyota on some models.

2. Ford's Focus received an award from the Insurance Institute for Highway Safety. The Focus earned the "Top Safety Pick" award for the 2009 model year.

3. Financially, Ford is making great strides. They were the only Detroit automotive manufacturer that stood on their own and did not rely on a government bailout to enable them to move forward.

From my perspective, these accomplishments are attributable to Ford's refocusing on the basic business principles of introducing fresh and innovative new products centered on customer wants and needs, while at the same time, improving the quality of their products. In addition, successful cost and debt reductions were implemented to further strengthen their financial position.

I don't think there is anything new other than the commitment to Ford's "focus." Their CEO, Alan Mulally, and the Ford team, have worked together and have proven that "laser" focus on the customer, on fresh products, on quality and on personal relationships add up to success.

More recently I had the opportunity, and the pleasure, of spending some time with Alan Mulally, the President and CEO of Ford Motor Company. I walked away from that meeting with a feeling of exhilaration, and a sense that here is a man with a vision. He knows where the company needs to go and he has the support of an enthusiastic team working together to get there.

To say that Alan Mulally is a man of great passion is putting it mildly. He goes beyond focused; he is laser focused. He exudes confidence, and at the same time, he's genuine and down to earth. Judging from his smile and the light in his eyes when he talks about the future of Ford, he likes what he is doing and he is having fun doing it.

From another perspective, as I approached the lobby of Ford's World Headquarters, I anticipated a "doom and gloom" atmosphere and low employee morale given all the negative comments and "catastrophic" outlook for the US auto industry during the previous few years. Not so at Ford! There was a bounce in everyone's step, and there were smiles on everyone's faces – all of which seemed to express, "I'm glad to be part of the Ford team." The comment I heard from many people was "Please ask him if he'll stay another ten years." Talk about a great relationship among the people.

Epilogue

To me, that summed it up. Alan Mulally has brought new focus and new ideas to Ford. Today there is an "esprit de corps" that I suspect has been missing for years. My take is that he is not just a visionary, but he is a man on a mission. He epitomizes all the characteristics of a true leader.

It goes beyond the man. It is readily apparent that there's a vision and a plan in place to support that vision. While I did not have enough time to survey the Ford team, as I stated in an article entitled, "Ford Proves That Basic Business Principles Still Work," I firmly believe the Ford plan embodies the following principles:

- It is focused on customer wants and needs
- Goals are integrated at each level of the organization to support the vision and to ensure that the plans of one area complement those of other areas
- Everyone is involved and informed

After speaking with Mr. Mulally, I am further convinced the Ford plan includes several other ingredients that will keep them on the path to success.

- It is predicated upon a team approach, and the team is committed to achieve the plan
- Every objective supports the overall plan goals and the vision
- Goals are based on specific and measurable data and outputs
- Specific responsibilities are assigned to people to ensure that planned actions are implemented
- There are scheduled progress reviews

It's working! Look at the trend of their quality indicators, customer satisfaction ratings and market share increases. They all are improving!

After the meeting, not only were my previous impressions of Ford's progress reinforced, but I walked away feeling renewed and reenergized about Ford's global presence now and in the future.

With Alan Mulally in the driver's seat, it should be quite a ride! I believe the Ford team is going to meet or exceed the expectations of its customers, its employees, its shareholders and its competitors by staying on plan and by achieving its vision.

Magna also has continued to do well, and today is one of the largest and most diversified automotive suppliers in the world. It has continued to grow profitably and has continued to expand its operations.

Led by Alan Mulally, the Ford team has continued to stay focused on their plan and Ford has reported several significant achievements along the way including:

- Selling Ford's Automotive Components Holdings (ACH) automotive headlight and taillight business and the Sandusky plant to Flex-N-Gate supply group.
- Sale of Ford's last ACH operation, the climate control operation located in their Sheldon Road Plant. This sale fulfilled ACH's strategy to exit ACH-managed component operations by selling them to key automotive suppliers.
- In August 2012, Ford marked a milestone by selling its 350 millionth vehicle.
- Another milestone in 2012 was achieved when the Ford Focus become the best selling nameplate in the world.
- In October 2012, the Board of Directors announce a fourth quarter dividend at the same level as was paid in each of the first three quarters of the year.

Finally, Ford and Magna are building on their prior alliance relationship. On March 20, 2009, CNNMoney.com posted the following article. "Ford is preparing to sell an electric car developed almost entirely by an outside supplier. While that may cut down on bragging rights—General Motors created the Chevy Volt in-house—it also cut down on costs and risk.

In other words, why invent the electric wheel when somebody else can do it for you? Meanwhile, Ford's partner, auto supplier Magna International, is offering to do for other carmakers what it's done for Ford and possibly more. If you're a carmaker and

Epilogue

you want to sell an electric car, Magna says it is ready to design it and build it for you. The electric Ford Focus ... is largely the product of Canada-based auto parts and assembly supplier Magna International."

To me this demonstrates that the parties took the best aspects of their prior relationship and continued to build upon their prior successes. The results are joint development of a new, leading edge, hi-tech vehicle which could help grow the US domestic automotive business. It also could help reduce our dependency on oil.

The results of this joint effort by Ford and Magna epitomize the fact that if people dedicate the time and effort necessary to build a lasting relationship, the benefits more than likely will exceed their original expectations.

It certainly is hard to argue with that.

www.ingramcontent.com/pod-product-compliance
Lightning Source LLC
Chambersburg PA
CBHW061512180526
45171CB00001B/145